SME Finance and the Economic Crisis

This book analyses the financing problems of Greek small and medium-sized enterprises (SMEs), within a liberalised financial system and within an economic environment of fiscal and monetary constraints. Using recent data covering a ten-year period, the main aim of the research is to explain the interdependence between the situation of the banking sector generally and that of SMEs.

The author argues that the reluctance of banks to lend to Greek companies because of the strict financing constraints due to the national debt crisis serves to exacerbate the cycle of economic recession. This factor seriously undermines the efforts of Greek companies to develop growth opportunities, and negatively affects their competitiveness as well as their ability to strengthen their market position. The author examines the supply and demand aspect of the problem: there is lower demand for lending due to the decline of demand for goods and services as well as a tightening of banks' credit standards, whilst on the supply side, the deteriorating financial situation of banks and their willingness to avoid increasing risk are important contributing factors. Finally, the author presents the main conclusions of the analyses carried out in the previous sections of the book and discusses some relevant recommendations for future research.

Building on the extant literature, this book analyses the problem from the point of view of both businesses and the banking sector. The study is useful for scholars, businesses, and policy decision makers who are interested in the problem of SMEs financing.

Alina Hyz, Ph.D., is a Professor of Business Administration at the Department of Accounting and Finance, University of West Attica, Athens, Greece. Her research interests are focused on Business Analysis, Strategy Development, Budgeting, and Finance.

Routledge Studies in the European Economy

Economic Crisis and Structural Reforms in Southern Europe
Policy Lessons
Edited by Paulo Manasse and Dimitris Katsikas

Crisis in the European Monetary Union
A Core-Periphery Perspective
Giuseppe Celi, Andrea Ginzberg, Dario Guarascio and Annamaria Simonazzi

Rethinking Economic and Monetary Union in Europe
A Post-Keynesian Alternative
Philip B. Whyman

Central and Eastern Europe in the EU
Challenges and Perspectives Under Crisis Conditions
Edited by Christian Schweiger and Anna Visvizi

Greek Employment Relations in Crisis
Problems, Challenges and Prospects
Edited by Horen Voskeritsian, Panos Kapotas and Christina Niforou

Centrally Planned Economies
Theory and Practice in Socialist Czechoslovakia
Edited by Libor Žídek

SME Finance and the Economic Crisis
The Case of Greece
Alina Hyz

For a full list of titles in this series, please visit www.routledge.com/series/SE0431

SME Finance and the Economic Crisis

The Case of Greece

Alina Hyz

Routledge
Taylor & Francis Group
LONDON AND NEW YORK

First published 2019
by Routledge
2 Park Square, Milton Park, Abingdon, Oxon OX14 4RN

and by Routledge
605 Third Avenue, New York, NY 10017

First issued in paperback 2020

Routledge is an imprint of the Taylor & Francis Group, an informa business

British Library Cataloguing-in-Publication Data
A catalogue record for this book is available from the British Library

Library of Congress Cataloging-in-Publication Data
Names: Hyz, Alina, author.
Title: SME finance and the economic crisis: the case of Greece / Alina Hyz.
Description: Abingdon, Oxon; New York, NY: Routledge, [2019] |
Series: Routledge studies in the European economy |
Includes bibliographical references and index.
Identifiers: LCCN 2019005166 | ISBN 9781138388123 (hardback)
Subjects: LCSH: Small business—Greece—Finance. | Financial crises—Greece.
Classification: LCC HD2346.G75 H99 2019 | DDC 338.4/30009495090512—dc23
LC record available at https://lccn.loc.gov/2019005166

ISBN 13: 978-0-367-72908-0 (pbk)
ISBN 13: 978-1-138-38812-3 (hbk)

Typeset in Times New Roman
by codeMantra

Contents

Figures

Tables

About the author

Alina Hyz is a professor of Business Administration at the Department of Accounting and Finance, University of West Attica, Athens, Greece. She studied economics at the University of Lodz and holds a PhD in Business Administration from the same university. Her research interests are focused on Business Analysis, Strategy Development, and Budgeting and Finance. She is the author of many research monographs and scientific articles in Greece and abroad. She has received invitations and delivered talks in various universities and institutions and major international conferences. She has professional and teaching experience: assistant professor at the University of Lodz, Poland (1988–1997), post-doctoral research fellowship from the Greek Ministry of Education at the University of Macedonia, Department of International and European Economic Studies, Thessaloniki, and Robert Schuman scholar at the European Parliament, Directorate General for Research, Luxembourg. She has been for many years a member of the Research Committee, editorial director of scientific journal *Review of Economic Sciences*, head of the Department of Accounting, TEI of Epirus (2005–2007, 2013), and more.

Preface

The SMEs are a crucial source of competitive development, economic growth, dynamism, and flexibility in major economies around the world. Financing is necessary to help them set up and expand their operations, develop new products, and invest in new employees or production facilities. In the fast-changing knowledge-based economy, the financial gap in SMEs is all the more critical because of the speed of innovation. Affordable and appropriate access to financing sources is an important issue not only for newly starting and growing companies, but also to the existing ones who wish to survive in the competitive environment. Unlike large firms, small businesses lack access to public institutional debt and equity capital markets, and the vicissitudes of small business profits make retained earnings a significantly less stable source of capital. In the bank-based financial system, bank credit is one of the primary sources of external financing for small business.

SMEs account for a significant share of the Greek economy regarding employment and value added. This share is among the highest in all European countries. Due to this, the economic situation of these enterprises has particularly important implication for the pace of Greek economy recovery and growth. During the last economic crisis debt financing had become more expensive and difficult to obtain. Since Greek SMEs can be classified as bank-dependent borrowers, credit channel effects were significantly most important to these firms. As a result, these firms suffer considerably from a contraction of credit. These enterprises have restricted access to external capital and hence, relatively few of them tap such capital relying mainly on their own funds. It limits their development opportunities, affects negatively the growth of their competitiveness, and the possibilities of strengthening their market position.

The extreme reluctance of banks to lend Greek companies because of the strict financing constraints due to the national debt crisis exacerbates the cycle of economic recession and seriously undermines the efforts of Greek companies to continue their activities. The small size of the Greek's SME accentuates their financing problem. There is no doubt that there are many factors which contribute to this decline. In this study, we examine the supply side and demand side of this problem. On the demand side, lower demand for lending by small firms due to the decline of demand on goods and services, generally bad financial position, and tightening of credit standards by banks which firms could not fulfil seems to be the most important. On the supply side, the deteriorating financial situation of banks and their willingness to avoid increasing risk are among the most important.

There are two main reasons behind the writing of this book. The first is related to the structural changes that the Greek banking sector witnessed over the last few years with the increased competition, mergers and acquisitions, and internationalisation activity. The most challenging period began with the eruption of the recent financial crisis. The Greek banking sector suffered significant blows in their levels of profitability, witnessed a sharp upturn of non-performing exposures, and struggled with record outflows of bank deposits. The recent financial crisis, in the case of Greece, leaves many unanswered questions regarding the lending behaviour of banks. As financial intermediaries, banks, on the one hand, generate profits and on the other, they create the growth of social welfare. In this process, they take risks related to their functioning. In times of crisis, there are some incentives to reduce risk. If this behaviour persists for an extended period, it can have adverse effects on social welfare by limiting the bank lending to businesses. The reduction of loans granted by banks adversely affects their profitability and creates unfavourable conditions for the functioning of economic units. Just as properly functioning of banking sector promotes growth, adverse financial conditions prevent a business sector from reaching its potential. It concerns especially countries such as Greece, where the vast majority of enterprises are SMEs for which bank financing is the only source of external funding. Although the problem of the influence of the crisis on banks is widely discussed in the relevant literature, there is no systematic research on bank lending, especially for individual countries. Despite the use of a common currency in the countries of the monetary union and single monetary policy, the experience of the recent crisis indicates the existence of significant differences between countries about the analysed problem.

The main aim of this research is to explain the interdependence between the situation of the banking sector and the situation of the most significant concerning employment and value added sector of the Greek economy, which is the sector of SMEs. Typically, researches concentrate on the problem of small businesses financing from the view of enterprises. This book tries to analyse the problem from the business point of view and the banking sector. Since the banking sector is the main source of SMEs financing in the stage of firms' growth, the emphasis is given to this stage of firm's development and not necessary on all firm's stages of development.

Since the study is destined for both academic and non-academic readers who are interested in the problem of SMEs, financing econometric calculations are not used. The data available in this research cover the period from 2006 to 2016. The book provides a balanced mix of theory and practice.

Although this study is based on collected data and numerical figures, it should be viewed as a qualitative study. This book includes six chapters.

The first chapter 'Sources of business capital' is a comprehensive analysis of the main sources of business financing. Looking at the features of the contemporary business environment, conclusions were made about the priorities of the efficient enterprise operation and the specific of financial decisions taken in it. An insight into the basic principles of the enterprise life cycle conception is provided. Thus, the chapter provides a framework for substantive research presented in the subsequent chapters.

The second chapter 'Small and medium enterprises in Greece' highlights the standard criteria and approaches used in the definition of SMEs. This chapter presents the latest empirical evidence concerning the situation of SMEs operating in Greece and in particular, compares and contrasts the position of SMEs in Greece and the EU before and after the recent financial crisis. It provides up-to-date evidence of the structure and contribution to employment and economic activity in the European context and, finally, analyse the main constraints preventing Greek SMEs from growing and generating more jobs and economic growth during the period under investigation.

The third chapter 'Why is bank lending so important in Greece?' describes the demand side and reports the results of the first research. After the short presentation of the so-called bank-based financial system, the analysis of data on small-business lending is provided. In this chapter, new evidence on how the financial crisis affected bank lending to SMEs in Greece is also presented.

The fourth chapter 'State of Greek banking sector: supply side' discusses the relevance and effectiveness of banking consolidation process in Greece in supporting SMEs priorities. This includes a summary of the available evidence as well as the results of the implementation of the rating system in the valuation of bank institutions in Greece.

The fifth chapter 'State of the business economy: profitability and dependence on debt' presents the results of the empirical analysis of the situation of the business economy in Greece. The aim of this chapter is twofold. First, it attempts to evaluate the profitability and business dependence on debt. Second, it purports to explore the relationship between determinants which are specific for firms and their capital structure. Data for the study were collected from the small and medium-sized sector in the region of Epirus in Greece.

The sixth chapter 'Recommendations and conclusions' contains concluding remarks and suggest points for discussion.

Alina Hyz
December 2018

Abbreviations

bn	billion
BLS	Bank Lending Survey
CAR	Capital Adequacy Ratio
EC	European Commission
ECB	European Central Bank
EIB	European Investment Bank
ELA	Emergency Liquidity Assistance
EMP	Electronic Means of Payment
EU	European Union
EU-28	the 28 EU Member States
EUR	Euro
GDP	Gross Domestic Product
HFSF	Hellenic Financial Stability Fund
HHI	Herfindahl-Hirshman Index
M&A	Mergers and Acquisitions
MFIs	Monetary Financial Institutions
NACE	Nomenclature Generale des Activites Economiques dans l'Union Europeene
NAICS	North American Industry Classification System
No.	number
NPE	Non-Performing Exposures
NPL	Non-Performing Loan
OECD	Organisation for Economic Co-operation and Development
ROA	Return on Assets
ROE	Return on Equity
SAFE	Survey on the Access to Finance of Enterprises
SBA	Small Business Act
SBS	Structural Business Statistics
SME	Small and Medium-Sized Enterprises
UK	United Kingdom
UN	United Nations

UNIDO	Industrial Development Organization of the United Nations
US	United States
USD	US dollar
WTO	World Trade Organization

1 Sources of business capital

1.1 Introduction

The analysis of the modern enterprise's environment is not an end in itself, in this chapter. However, the changes in the company's environment, especially in the external environment, have a significant impact on the enterprise's decision-making process. These changes can support or obstruct the company's operation and development. They may apply to all sectors of the economy or only to some of them. They create a heterogeneous set of phenomena, within which it is possible to isolate global, structural, and institutional processes, concerning the sphere of production and technology. Among the factors determining the firm's operation and growth, and its decision-making process, two groups can be distinguished. The first includes factors that are relatively easy to control by the company. They are known as internal factors. The second group contains those factors that are usually beyond the influence of manager's control. These second group of factors can be treated as external conditions for the operation and development of enterprises.

Internal and external factors affect a company's capital structure with a greater or lesser intensity in different periods. The optimal capital structure requires appropriate proportions between equity and debt, which leads to a balance between return and risk. These proportions depend on the environment. As the environment is changing, the optimal capital structure must also be changed. The unambiguous influence of these factors is difficult to determine even with complex financial management techniques. The multiplicity and variability of the environment make determining the optimal capital structure difficult.

This chapter provides a framework for substantive research presented in the subsequent chapters. In this chapter, we try to find answers to the following questions: Which are the main characteristics of the contemporary business environment? Which are the primary sources of business capital? Which are the factors affecting the availability and choice of funding sources for small and medium-sized enterprises (SMEs) in different phases of their life?

1.2 Main features of the contemporary business environment

The environment of a modern business becomes more and more complex. Changes that we can observe affect the functioning of all social systems. Among them are SMEs. Perhaps the most important features that affect the functioning of SMEs at the beginning of the twenty-first century are:

1 Unprecedented structural uncertainty.
2 Internationalisation of markets and the decline of national borders.
3 Globalisation in the sphere of economy.
4 Intensification of integration processes.
5 Rapid intensification of global competition between firms.
6 Intensification of technological progress that caused substantial changes in job organisation, management methods, and methods of production.
7 Increasing the use of modern information and communication systems in management.

Uncertainty is placed on the list of the main characteristics of contemporary social and economic systems as a component of the triad: the complexity of the system, its dynamics, and uncertainty. Certainty is characterised by complete information about each course of action and the advanced knowledge that each alternative has a unique outcome. Uncertainty is characterised by imperfect knowledge about each alternative and the expectation that each alternative has two or more possible outcomes. Uncertainty can be considered in three basic dimensions: the lack of information necessary to make decisions, the inability to predict the effects of decisions, and finally, the inability to estimate the effects of events taking place in the environment. The complexity of the environment and the speed of changes taking place in it are a source of uncertainty for the organisation. Uncertainty in this context means that the participants of the organisation perceive the environment as unpredictable (Ferrari-Filho and Conceicao, 2005). Organisations, due to the turbulence occurring in their environment, function in the so-called 'structural uncertainty' in which survival requires coordination, adaptation skills, and anticipation of what will happen. At this point, it is important to notice the difference between uncertainty and risk. A risk may be defined as the phenomenon that arises from circumstances where we can identify the possible outcomes and even their probability of occurrence without being sure which will occur.[1] Uncertainty describes the situation where we are not able to identify all the possible outcomes and still less able to assess their probability of occurrence.

Particularly noteworthy phenomena in the contemporary environment are the ongoing globalisation process. This process is complicated and multilateral. It covers several aspects and processes, and involves many countries and societies (Frankel, 2000; Chang and Lee, 2010). As a result, it leads to the creation of a more and more homogeneous world system. Liberalisation of trade on a global scale, in turn, forces enterprises to look for new ways of efficient competition, when the advantage based on privileged access to basic resources such as cheap labour and raw materials loses its importance. The opening of markets on the international and global scale is a factor that stimulates the development of enterprises. Economic growth, development of technologies, unification of tastes, and requirements of clients in various countries contribute to the gradual disappearance of barriers in the form of state borders for the operations of companies.

A characteristic feature of the contemporary environment is also the tendency to integrate. An example is the creation of the EU. Functioning in the EU means, among other things, the free movement of goods, services, capital, and people as well as increased competition, improving the quality of the market offer, and changing the standards of social life. Consequently, it should, at least in theory, lead to sustainable economic development. This effect may be achieved, among others, through supporting the efficient allocation of production resources, enabling mass production, creating incentives to develop innovation.

The main effects of globalisation and integration processes are the intensification of competition between enterprises with unprecedented development of knowledge and technological progress (Romer, 1986; Odagiri, 1994; Baylis et al., 2014). The development of knowledge and the importance of intellectual capital enable searching for unique ways of gaining a competitive advantage based on technological and organisational innovations. Technological progress affects the production process and its competitiveness, and it determines the level of profits and shapes the organisation's resources, including knowledge and skills (Fusari, 2016, 2017). The continuous technological changes of unprecedented speed in the environment of contemporary enterprises may constitute a threat or opportunity for the organisation. If the organisation ignores them, they form a threat, whereas if they are anticipated, they may create an opportunity for the organisation's development.

The challenges of modern economy force enterprises to take a new look at the nature and value of information. Today, information has measurable value in the form of material benefits for the enterprises. Often, the information is more valuable than the product of human hands or machines. The development of modern information and communication technologies, and hence fast, cheap, and accurate acquisition of information, leads to its broad application and opens new opportunities for enterprises.

Particular attention, due to the subject of this study, deserves the processes occurring in the contemporary financial markets. Characteristic trends for these markets are their dynamics and increased interdependence between financial markets; globalisation of financial markets and internationalisation of business and markets as well as increased risk and instability of financial markets (Hefferman, 2005; Kose et al., 2007; Beck et al., 2009). The risk of international financial markets has always existed, and there is no indication that it will be limited in the future. On the contrary, the risk of financial markets is growing, and from time to time, it makes itself felt through emerging financial crises. Globalisation, new financial instruments, and increasing interdependence of markets and instruments cause an increase in risk. One of the most critical issues caused by the process of globalisation in the international financial system is the increased threat to global financial stability (Mundell, 1995; Mishkin, 1999). At the same time, new financial instruments and securitisation allow the transfer of risk from one market to another, as we could observe during the last financial crisis in 2008. The global economy has dynamics of development, which contains the risk of destabilisation associated with the unevenness of growth rate and changes in the structure of the economy and financial markets (Chant, 2003; Schinazi, 2004; Allen and Wood, 2006). As recent experiences show, countries and markets are increasingly interlinked. Difficulties that arise in one country in one sector can easily spread to other areas and cross-national borders.

All the above changes are forcing the enterprises to treat the essential characteristics of the modern environment, such as variability, complexity, uncertainty as natural, and concerning all organisations (although in different intensity and time).

What is the impact of these changes on the functioning of modern SMEs? They undoubtedly increase the opportunities and threats to their operation and development. Therefore, they must continuously identify changes and adapt to them. In other words, the analysis of the environment must constitute a fundamental condition for the efficient functioning of modern SMEs. The results of this analysis must be used in the decision-making process. Only in this way these firms may survive, develop, and create a competitive advantage.

1.3 Enterprises' financial decisions: general remarks

Financial decisions constitute a particular example of the decision taken in enterprises. The fundamental financial decisions include investment decisions, financing decisions, and dividend decisions. The necessity to make the investment decision results from the fact that the resources of every enterprise are limited, and therefore, it is necessary to locate them to maximise the utility and achieve the highest rate of return. Investment decisions include the selection of assets. The company puts its funds in fixed assets and current assets. Financing decision is vital to make a business acquire fund. They cover the choice of financing sources for the company. Finally, dividend decisions relate to the distribution of profits earned by the organisation. The primary alternatives are whether to distribute the earnings. Dividend policy influences, in the long run, the ability of the firm to finance its investments from own sources.

Financial decisions are made based on several factors that determine them (Figure 1.1). The most important factors include macroeconomic factors,

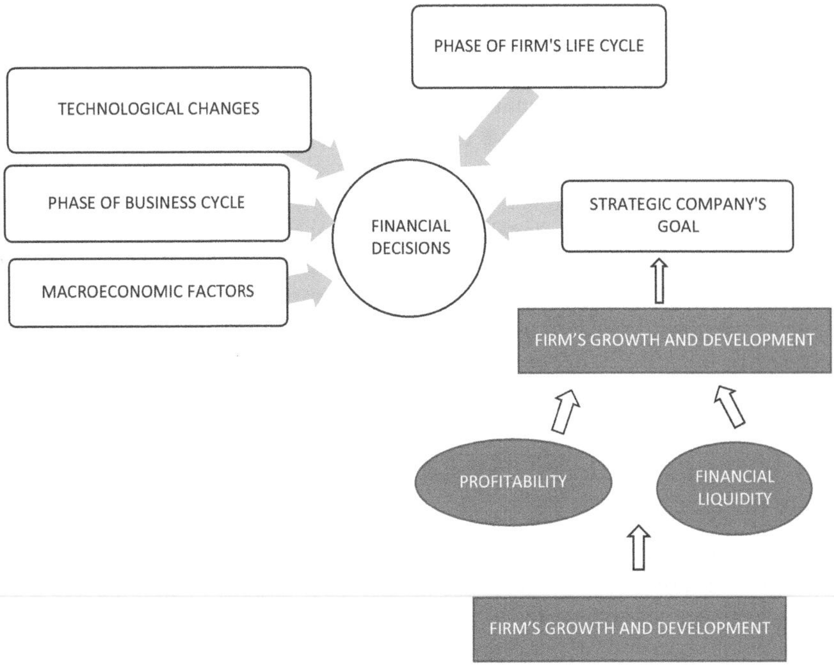

Figure 1.1 Financial decisions – conceptual framework.
Source: Author's work.

phases of the business cycle, and technological changes. The macroeconomic factors shape the capital flow and hence, significantly determine the company's ability to obtain external financing sources. The business cycle phase also affects the financial situation of the company. For example, the development phase generally has a positive effect on the financial condition of the company, whereas the crisis or recession phase has negative effect. Rapid technological changes force enterprises to invest more and, consequently, to seek sources of their financing. Analysing the specificity of enterprises, it should be emphasised that financial decisions are dependent to a large extent on the phase of the firm's life cycle. Section 1.5 provides the basic principles of the enterprise life cycle conception. The individual phases of the life cycle are characterised by a different firm's size and resources. The fundamental factors that determine the choice of funding sources and shape the capital structure in individual phases of the life cycle are a risk level, development opportunities, and financial surplus. Financial decisions are also conditioned by the characteristics of the company, such as the type of activities, legal form, and competitive position.

Another determinant of financial decisions is the strategic goal of the company. What is the strategic goal of the company? There is a widespread view that the firm's goal is a long-run survival. The condition for a firm's survival is to ensure sustainable profitability and obtain financial liquidity. Survival can be considered as the company's main goal in a crisis when the company threatens to collapse. Under normal conditions, it is regarded as a preliminary objective, enabling the implementation of other purposes. In a dynamic and competitive environment, the firm's growth and development can be a condition of survival. Growth- and development-oriented decisions are very complex. First, they are characterised by long-term nature and the need to develop a secure financial basis. An enterprise's financial resources determine the possibilities of investment projects realisation and, therefore, its development opportunities. However, the access to the funding sources also determines the current operation of the company because it decides, among other things, about the enterprise's financial liquidity.

1.4 Internal and external financing sources: main findings from the literature review

It is not possible to start and continue operation of a business without adequate financial resources. Their use is related to the creation of a specific financial structure that can affect both the current financial condition of the company and its value. The company's financing sources are visible on the liabilities side of the balance sheet of the business unit. They may be divided into different categories depending on the criteria we use. According to the duration of use, we can distinguish long-term financing sources, which are involved and necessary to return throughout one year from their acquisition, and short-term financing sources, which are acquired by the company for less than one year of use. When they are generated from the current activity of the company, they belong to the internal sources of financing. Internal financing sources are also referred to as self-financing. When they are obtained from the financial environment of the enterprise, they create an external source of financing. Firms can choose from a range of external financing instruments, in particular, equity, bank loans, debt securities, inter-company loans, and trade credit. This opportunity of choice provides them with flexibility in their decision of financing of working capital and investment (Storey, 1994; Berger and Udell, 1998). According to the use of capital, they are divided into fixed capital, which includes equity and long-term liabilities, and working capital financing current assets of the enterprise. These are primarily short-term liabilities.

Proper determination of the value of assets and share of equity and debt plays a vital role in the rational use of the company's capital resources. Mutual relations between the structure of assets and sources of financing result mainly from the specific nature of the company's operations and the nature of the industry in which it operates.

Depending on mutual balance relations, two groups of rules are distinguished:

- The rules of the horizontal structure of the capital and assets.
- The rules of the vertical structure of capital.

Within the horizontal capital's and assets' structure, we can analyse:

- The golden funding rule (banking or classic), according to which debt should be fully covered by equity.
- The golden balance sheet rule, which requires that fixed assets which are characterised by a low degree of liquidity should be fully financed with equity. The broader approach assumes financing fixed assets and part of current assets with the company's fixed capital, that is, equity and long-term liabilities.

The vertical structure of capital expresses only the shaping of the right proportions of equity and debt in the company's balance sheet. In practice, adherence to the golden balance sheet rule decreases the financial risk and guarantees maintaining of the financial balance of the company. This has the effect of increasing the company's financial credibility and determining the optimal capital structure.

Debt constitutes 'preferential' capital that has priority over equity at the time of liquidation or bankruptcy. The debt financing brings potential benefits related to tax shields and financial leverage. The tax shield reduces the taxable base by paying interest, which is the tax-deductible cost, and therefore reduces the mandatory financial result burden. Leverage, in turn, increases the return on equity by introducing debt financing with a lower interest rate than the return on investment (ROI).

Capital structure is defined as the relative amount of debt and equity employed by a firm to fund a business operation, capital expenditures, acquisitions, and other investments. The structure can be expressed as a debt-to-equity ratio or debt-to-capital ratio. There are two main types of firms as far as capital structure is considered: unleveraged firms and levered firms. Unleveraged firms raise the capital from sources like retained earnings and equity, and levered firms use a mix of equity, retained earnings and various forms of debt.

Capital structure and the rules and principles of its shaping are issues studied by many authors. These studies attempt to identify factors affecting the capital structure and, on this basis, attempt to formulate theories that adequately explain the behaviour of enterprises. There are various capital structure theories trying to establish a relationship between the financial leverage of a company with its market value, but there is no universal theory of the debt-equity choice.

In 1958, Modigliani and Miller proposed the theory of irrelevance of capital structure (Modigliani and Miller, 1958). This theory is based on very restrictive assumptions, like perfect capital markets, homogenous expectations, no taxes, and no transaction costs. These assumptions do not hold in the real world. With the above assumptions, capital structure does not influence a firm's value and the cost of capital. Modigliani and Miller's tax model (The Tradeoff Theory of Leverage) acknowledges tax savings and thus infers that a change in the debt-equity ratio influences weighted average cost of capital (Modigliani and Miller, 1963; Miller, 1977). This means, higher the debt, lower is the weighted average cost of capital. In other words, the trade-off theory advocates that a company can capitalise its requirements with debts if the cost of distress exceeds the value of tax benefits. It means that the company may set a target level of leverage at which tax advantages caused by the increase of the debt just offset the cost arising from potential financial distress. Thus, the leverage can increase a firm's value, and firms have to trade-off between the costs of financial distress, agency costs, and tax benefits to have an optimal capital structure. However, it is worth noting that the existence of an excellent or optimal capital structure is controversial. It is generally accepted that as the use of borrowed funds by an enterprise increases, the higher the probability of bankruptcy. However, the company's problems start to appear long before the company is in the process of bankruptcy. These problems, which are created due to excessive borrowing, are known as financial distress and have a significant impact on the company's activities. Business executives may have different goals than the primary and objective purpose of the business. For example, they can seek to increase their earnings or avoid investment projects that offer high returns, but they also have a high risk. Therefore, the managers of a business are not perfect representatives of its shareholders. Shareholders and lenders must take control measures to prevent managers from making decisions solely for the benefit of their own. The cost of these controls is known in financial theory as agency costs, that is, costs borne by owners of the firm resulting from potential conflicts between managers, debt holders, and equity holders (Jensen, 1986; Harris and Raviv, 1991). The agency cost is related to the company's capital structure and the relationship between shareholders and the lender. Loan funds are most often provided with certain restrictive covenants. Indicative examples are restrictions on the additional borrowing burden on the company. The existence of restrictive terms limits the effectiveness of the firm's activity. The reduction in efficiency and the required management controls have an agency cost that is passed on to the company's shareholders through the increase in the cost of borrowed funds and the decrease in the company's share price. This reduces the advantages of using loans.

The pecking order theory (Donaldson, 1961; Myers, 1984; Myers and Majluf, 1984) explains how asymmetrical information can influence a capital structure and suggests that firms hierarchically finance their needs. Due to adverse selection, firms prefer internal to external finance, and they use external sources only when the internal is exhausted. If external funds are necessary, firms prefer debt to new equity because debt financing entails lower information costs. In other words, this theory suggests that there tends to be a hierarchy in firms' preferences for financing: first using internally available funds, followed by debt, and finally external equity. Therefore, most companies fund their activities first with retained earnings and depreciation, and then borrowed funds, and only if they have exhausted all other sources of funding, they use new equity. This finding is in contradiction with the trade-off theory model, which, as we have mentioned before, assumes that the retained earnings do not differ in any way from the new equity. Myers (1984) concluded that this difference is because the trade-off model does not consider that some market participants have better information than others. This view is known as the asymmetric information theory of the capital structure. This theory assumes that managers have more information about a firm than potential debt or equity holders. These informational asymmetries cause difficulties when potential creditors and equity holders try to evaluate the prospects of different firms. The effect of these information problems is to boost the cost of external finance comparing the cost of internal finance (Akerlof, 1970; Greenwald and Stiglitz, 1990, Myers and Majluf, 1984; Aggarwall and Zong, 2006). Companies will only need to issue new equity in two cases: the first is when companies have no other way to finance their investment projects, and the second, if they believe that the stock prices of the shares of their business are overvalued. Investors view the announcement of issuing new equity as a signal of the prospects of the company. The result of this signal is that the price of a share frequently falls after the announcement of the issue of new equity. The asymmetric information theory suggests that companies should retain a significant part of their earnings and keep a relatively low debt-to-equity ratio. In other words, maintain a reserve borrowing capacity. It allows the company to cover future investment programmes with additional loans without being obliged to issue new equity.

Empirical studies based on these theories identify many factors which determine a company's capital structure. Some of them are firm-specific, others industry-specific, and the last group covers country-specific institutional factors. These factors are denoted profitability, opportunity or rate of growth, the tangibility of assets or assets structure, non-debt tax shields, uniqueness, industry classification, earnings volatility, business risk, ownership structure, and firm's size. Most empirical evidence on capital structure tends to focus on large firms. Some authors analyse separate measures of short-term, long-term, and convertible debt rather than an aggregate measure of total debt.

Several researchers have tested the effects of profitability on firm leverage. The results are ambiguous. On the one hand, the trade-off theory suggests that profitable firms should borrow more to take tax advantages, and on the other, firms with lower profitability should borrow less because of bankruptcy costs[2] and because the fixed obligation of interest payments could seriously hinder their situation. So, in this case, we have a positive relationship between profitability and the firm's leverage. On the opposite, the pecking order theory suggests that firms will use retained earnings first as investment funds, and subsequently move to debt and new equity only if necessary. In this case, there would be a negative relationship between profitability and leverage (Kester, 1986; Titman and Wessels, 1988; Rajan and Zingales, 1995; Wald, 1999; Fama and French, 2002; Abor, 2005) and more profitable firms will be less leveraged and the less profitable more leveraged. In this case, small and medium-sized firms due to their features will be less leveraged (Michaelas et al., 1999; Fama and French, 2002).

Firms with high growth opportunities have more significant needs for new sources of funding. In general, it is difficult to construct any proxy for a firm's growth opportunities. Most simple indicators include sales growth (Pandey, 2001), market-to-book ratio (Chen and Zhao, 2006), research and development expenses (R&D) (Titman and Wessels, 1988), and capital expenditures over total assets and growth of total assets measured by the percentage change in total assets. The theory predicts that firms with more investments have less leverage because they have strong incentives to avoid underinvestment and asset substitution inefficiencies that can arise from the stockholder-bondholder agency problems (Awan et al., 2010). Pecking order theory suggests that growth opportunities are negatively related to long-term debt levels. However, Myers (1977) argued that the agency problem could be mitigated if long-term debt is replaced by short-term debt. This suggests that the short-term debt ratio might be positively related to growth rate if growing firms substitute short-term financing for long-term financing.

As far as firm size is considered, the implicit anticipation is that large firms should have higher debt ratios and small firms should opt for lower debt levels (López-Gracia and Sogorb-Mira, 2008). The degree of asymmetric information and agency costs depends on firm characteristics. External funds tend to be relatively more expensive to smaller firms' providers of finance that have less information about their creditworthiness (Fazzari et al., 1988). Large firms are characterised by more stable cash flow and lower probability of bankruptcy. So, a positive relationship between leverage and size may occur. According to Smith (1977) and Titman and Wessels (1988), the cost of issuing debt and equity securities is also related to firm size. Small firms pay much more than large firms to issue new equity and long-term debt. This suggests that small firms may prefer to borrow short-term loans (through banks) rather than issue long-term debt because of the lower fixed costs associated with this alternative

An important role is played by the proportion of tangible assets in the total asset. Tangibility should be directly proportional to the level of debt that the company can afford, given the requirement of collateralised loans. Both the theory of financial distress and agency theory propounds that tangibility has a positive relation to capital structure. According to the theory of financial distress, if a firm has a high proportion of tangible assets that can be used as collateral may expect to issue more debt than a firm with high proportion of intangible assets, because the former has lower costs of financial distress in the case of bankruptcy (Jensen and Meckling, 1976; Myers and Majluf, 1984).

Higher business risk increases the probability of financial distress. So, firms have to trade-off between tax benefits and bankruptcy costs. Thus, it predicts a negative relationship between business risk and leverage. Queen and Roll (1987) argue that SMEs are likely to have a higher level of business risk relative to large firms.

Titman and Wessels (1988) examine uniqueness as a determinant of a firm's capital structure. He proposed the following measures of uniqueness: expenditures on research and development over sales (RD/S); selling expenses over sales (SEIS); and quit rates (QR), that is, the percentage of the industry's total workforce that voluntarily left their jobs in the sample years. In his research, uniqueness is expected to be negatively related to debt ratios because customers, workers, and suppliers of firms that produce unique or specialised products probably suffer relatively high costs if they liquidate.

As far as industry classification is considered, Titman (1982) suggests that firms that make products requiring the availability of specialised servicing and spare parts will find liquidation especially costly. This indicates that firms manufacturing machines and equipment should be financed with relatively less debt.

One of the principal research priorities in international literature is an attempt to apply capital structure theory to SMEs. What main aspects which distinguish small and medium-sized firms from large enterprises affect the financial decisions of these firms? As La Rocca et al. (2011) concluded in their research on informational opacity and connected with its verification, adverse selection and moral hazard is the main factor which determines the possibilities of use of debt and external equity sources.

BOX 1.1 ASYMMETRIC INFORMATION

Information is crucial for an effective decision-making process for all economic units. The theorists of management consider information as the base for solving relevant managerial problems at micro and macro levels. Accountants deem information as a significant factor for firms' and financial markets' operations, and thus, they focus on finding specific accounting systems to record all essential information accurately and assure its quality. Gale (2006) highlights the necessity of accurate information on the economic performance of firms that may not only assist them in their operations, but also help the participants of financial markets to organise environmental risk management strategies, which can play a critical role in the proper functioning of financial markets. According to Lorraine et al. (2004), the disclosures of information concerning the good or poor environmental performance of firms ultimately affect their share prices and financial position. One significant drawback is the asymmetric nature of information between firms and other participants of the markets such as stock exchanges, the banking sector, investors, and insurance companies. Asymmetric information may be described as the study of decisions in transactions where one party has more or better information than the other. The problem of asymmetric information is not new. Neoclassical economics have recognised that information is not perfect. George Akerlof, in his famous 1970 article 'The Market for Lemons', succinctly described the problem of how low-quality used cars (lemons) drive high-quality used vehicles out of the market. New institutional economics explain why such an imperfection creates problems. Ronald Coase (1937) argued that there is transaction cost in acquiring information, negotiating, monitoring, signing, and enforcing contracts. Considering the firm not only as a system itself, but also as a part of economic macro-system, one can find the so-called 'decision' in cases of informational asymmetry. In situations of asymmetric information, the allocation of resources will not be economically efficient. When the distribution of information is asymmetric, one or more parties will have imperfect information and hence, bear the risk. The asymmetry can be resolved directly through appraisal or indirectly through screening, signalling, or contingent payments. Screening is an initiative of the party with less information, while signalling is an initiative of the party with better information.

The most significant benefit to the discipline of the economics of information is possibly the Stiglitz research on screening techniques (Stiglitz, 2001), used by one economic agent to extract otherwise private information from another agent. Screening involves strategies used by different organisations to avoid potentially disastrous decision-making complications in cases of asymmetric information.

Another case of asymmetric information applies to corporate firms and risk information in their annual reports. Adequate risk information may reduce uncertainty, help investors make informed investment decisions, and consequently reduce agency problems. The actual screening process not only depends on the nature of the scenario, but it is also connected with the future relationship between the parties. Equity market works using statements and published financial and other data made available by the company as public information. This forms the base information on which price of equity is determined.

In an ideal case of perfect and symmetric information being available to all the parties in the market using the same tools, everybody arrives at the same price for the equity. However, in practice, there is never perfect symmetric information available about the equity. Parties with some additional information about the equity will come up with a new estimate for the price of equity, and hence, there will be a trade of equity. Equity market functionality is thus based on the assumption that there is asymmetric information in the market, and therefore, every investor will have different views about the price of equity.

BOX 1.2 MORAL HAZARD: A PARTICULAR CASE OF INFORMATION ASYMMETRY

Economists explain moral hazard as a particular case of information asymmetry. Moral hazard may occur if a party that is insulated from risk has more information about its actions and intentions than the party paying for the negative consequences of the risk. More broadly, moral hazard occurs when the party with more information about its actions or intentions has a tendency or incentive to behave inappropriately from the perspective of the party with less information. It is easy to implement theories of asymmetric information and moral hazard to the problem of small and medium-sized business lending. Asymmetric information makes possible for banks to discriminate between healthy more easily and no healthy borrowers, and the so-called 'lemons' borrowers will be charged an extra risk premium or will be required to provide more collateral (Wang, 2008). SMEs have a higher probability to be viewed as 'lemons' because their information is opaque. Simultaneously, when risk significantly increased during the period of the financial crisis, banks became more reluctant to lend to SMEs with poor information availability. As a result, SMEs in imperfect capital markets have a higher probability to be financially constrained (Hubbard, 1995).

1.5 Financial life's cycle theory

The firm's life cycle model has attracted considerable attention in recent decades. It is often used as a conceptual framework for analysing various aspects of firm development. By applying the model, researchers try to investigate the firm's financial performance, strategy, organisational structure, entrepreneurship, leadership, profitability, liquidity, capital, and financial structure. Life cycle model can help researchers and practitioners to predict potential problems and opportunities which may occur in different firms' life stages.

The life cycle model is based on the concepts coming from the biological sciences. This development process can also be likened to the product life cycle. Like products, businesses do not move through the cycle at the same speed, but unlike most products, companies can stay in the same stage for a considerable period (Scott and Bruce, 1987). According to the life cycle model, a firm develops through various stages. The number of stages and substages identified by different scholars varies significantly (O'Farrell and Hitchens, 1988). In general, models varying from three to ten stages describe a similar pattern of development of organisation (Lester et al., 2003). The ultimate determination of how many stages a model proposes is how the researcher defines a life cycle stage (Hanks, 1990). Typically, the life cycle consists of a set of stages that starts with birth and ends with death. Regardless of how many stages of a company's life are identified by individual researchers, it is generally accepted that the duration of the different stages varies widely across industries and differs among individual companies. As accurately indicated by Scott and Bruce (1987), '(...) it is important to remember that the shape of the curve and the speed at which the firm moves through each stage will vary from business to business'. Also, not every company will go through every stage, and not all companies will succeed as a result of these stages (Lester and Parnell, 1999). Unlike living organisms, companies may be reborn, and declining does not necessarily mean the collapse of the enterprise.

In the literature, many concepts of the firm's life cycle can be found. Some of them are relevant to the industries, others to large businesses or all organisations (general models), and still others are tailored to the specificity of SMEs. Main researchers who have contributed to the development of the firm's life cycle concept are Chandler (1962), Churchill and Lewis (1983), Greiner (1972), Scott and Bruce (1987), Lester and Parnell (1999), and Hanks (1993).

Regardless of the authors' approach, the company's life cycle models outline the differences between the stage of the emergence of a new enterprise on the market, changes occurring in the period of growth or expansion and the situation of a mature enterprise. The main differences between the models mentioned above are as follows:

1 Some authors distinguish the stage preceding the birth of the enterprise, that is, the preconditioning phase.
2 In some models, the last distinguished phase of development is the maturity or stabilisation of the enterprise, while in others the negative aspect related to the end of the life cycle, that is, the collapse or 'death', of the enterprise is emphasised.

3 The third variant visible in some concepts is the restructuring phase, giving the chance of a 'rebirth' of the enterprise.
4 Most of the models stand out as the 'growth' stage of the company's development, while 'survival' was treated as a development phase.

According to Churchill and Lewis (1983), small businesses vary widely in size, management styles, organisational structures, and capacity for growth. But they experience common problems arising at similar stages in their development. The understanding of these stages allows us to analyse the nature, characteristics, and problems of businesses. Churchill and Lewis try to develop a framework relevant to small and growing businesses. They delineate the five stages of development. Each stage is characterised by an index of size, dispersion, and complexity, and described by five management factors: managerial style, organisational structure, the extent of formal systems, primary strategic goals, and the owner's involvement in the business. The model distinguishes five successive stages of the organisation's life: existence, survival, success, take-off, and resource maturity. It was established that whether the organisation develops and passes through successive stages is determined by the evolution of enterprise and management factors. These factors are financial resources (cash and financial capabilities), operational and strategic capabilities of the owner to operate, quality and diversity of staff, strategic planning, and formal procedures. Since the organisation at each stage is struggling with other problems and challenges, the role of individual factors changes.

Stage I is an existence. At this stage, the company's activities are determined by the owner-manager. Initially, the owner can even act alone. During this time, he builds a simple, uncomplicated organisation in which he initiates all processes and provides the necessary resources. Systems and formal planning are minimal to non-existent. The company's strategy is to take advantage of emerging opportunities, and the primary goal is to survive and stay in the market.

Further development will depend mainly on the sector in which the company started its operations as well as financial resources of the company's owner. If the company does not gain enough customer acceptance or product capability to become viable, the owners close the business when the start-up capital runs out and, eventually, sell the company for its asset value. In this start-up phase, two key factors are indicated as crucial: owner's operational abilities and financial resources. Lack of financial resources, as well as insufficient involvement of the owner in such areas as marketing, production, and management, contributes to the bankruptcies of many young companies. However, if the company's offer (products, services) will gain recognition and acceptance of customers, the company can stay on the market and go to the next stage of survival.

Stage II – Survival. Enterprises that have come to Stage II are usually well recognisable on the market. The organisation is still simple. The company may have a limited number of employees supervised by a sales manager or a general foreman. The owner still has a significant impact on the functioning of the enterprise and strongly identifies with it. At the same time, the primary goal is still survival and the owner is still synonymous with the business. The critical problem thus shifts from mere existence to the relationship between revenues and expenses. There are two main issues in this stage. The first one is the generation of cash to break even and to cover the repair or replacement of capital assets. And the second one is the generation of cash flow and to finance growth to a size that is sufficiently large to earn an economic return on assets and labour. Enterprises at this stage should introduce a system of formal planning with an emphasis on the cash forecasting. The main problem of these young companies is the ability to generate income. If the enterprises grow in the survival stage in size and profitability, it has a chance to move to the next stage – success. Or it may, as many companies do, remain at the survival stage for some time, earning marginal returns on invested time and capital, and eventually go out of business when the owner gives up or retires. In the case of these marginal businesses, the owner can sell the company, usually at a light loss. Other entities that failed to develop properly concerning organisational and economic disappear from the market – they are bankrupt or liquidated.

Stage III (success). In stage three, the decision facing owners is whether to exploit the company's accomplishments and use the company as a platform for growth and expand or keep the company stable and profitable, providing a base for alternative owner activities.

In the success-disengagement substage, the company has enough size, good economic position, and earnings above average. At the stage of success, the owner's strategic skills become more and more important. This is manifested in the owner's readiness to delegate duties to functional managers and build the organisational structure. If all conditions are met, the company will develop.

The growth of the company is associated with the implementation of new investments that should be preceded by a thorough analysis of the market, the company's capabilities, its weaknesses, and its strengths. Investments, in turn, require additional capital from internal or external sources. The second path at the stage of success is the owner's involvement in the activity. This is possible in organisations that dominate on the small but stable segments of the market, in which further development opportunities are limited, have reached appropriate sizes, and generate medium profits. Such companies can survive for a long time at the stage of success if adverse conditions in the company's environment do not appear. The owner can also sell or merge at a profit. If the enterprise does not adapt to changing market conditions, it may go bankrupt or go back to a marginally surviving company. In turn, organisations that manage to adapt to changed market conditions may move towards expansion, provided that any significant organisational changes are made. The main task at this stage is to stop the outflow of financial resources because a possible increase in expenses may bring the firm's bankruptcy. However, it may happen that the local market will not allow further development of the company and may remain at this stage for a long time.

In the success-growth substage, the owner consolidates the company and marshals' resources for growth. One of the most critical tasks is to make sure that the company stays profitable. Another task is to develop managers to meet the needs of the growing business with abilities of strategic management. If the company is successful, in this stage, it proceeds to Stage IV. If the substage of growth is unsuccessful, the causes may be detected in time for the company to shift to the success-disengagement stage. If not, retrenchment to the survival stage may be possible before bankruptcy or a distress sale.

Formal procedures and strategic planning become more and more critical after Stage IV (Take off) has passed those enterprises which have managed to grow further at the stage of success and have created a complex organisation. The organisational structure is expanded, specialised functional divisions are created. The desirable direction of development of structures is decentralisation with the involvement of competent managers. The owner is no longer able to manage the organisation on his own and his responsibilities are taken over by functional managers. In this stage, the key problems are how to grow rapidly and how to finance that growth. This stage often requires a willingness on the owner's part to tolerate a high debt-equity ratio at the stage of expansion; the most important factors for the company are management quality, strategic and operational planning, formal procedures, and the owner's strategic abilities to manage. Again, financial resources are gaining significance just like in the stage of existence and survival. They are to ensure the company's further development, which requires, among others, strict cost control and proper recognition of investment directions. Since there are so many critical factors in this stage, several scenarios may occur. If the owner rises to the challenges of a growing company, it can become a big business. If not, it can usually be sold at a profit after a short-term decline. If the company fails, it may be able to continue as a successful and substantial company at a state of equilibrium or it may drop back to Stage III or even to the survival stage or fail. The lack of strategic ability of the owner, poor quality of staff, and lack of strategic planning as well as formal procedures regulating the operation of the organisation can be indicated as the cause of failures. The causes of a company's failure in this stage can also be found in the rapid development of the enterprise, with limited access to finance.

The last and fifth stage in the model of development of SMEs is the maturity of the organisation. The main task in this stage controls the financial gains brought on by rapid growth. The company diversifies its operations by entering new markets, expanding its business profile. Therefore, the organisational structure is undergoing evolution, in which more and more space is available for managers, analysts, and advisers. Professional management tools, those related to the strategic planning process, budgets, management by objectives, and standard cost systems become more important. The owner and the business are quite separate, both financially and operationally. The main emphasis should be placed on controlling financial income and proper reinvestment of profits. If the financial results are not satisfactory for the owners, the unit may be sold or taken over by another entity. An essential threat at this stage is the loss of entrepreneurial spirit, which until now has 'driven' the company to act, triggered innovation, and encouraged risky activities. As a result, the company may be characterised by a lack of innovative decision-making and the avoidance of risks. However, if there is a significant regrouping of resources, there is a chance to go back to Stage IV – expansion and further development.

The analysis of the Churchill and Lewis' five stages of the life cycle of a SME leads to the observation that there are some factors related to the enterprise and some to the owner factors which are important in the company's development. Among the first, group financial resources, including cash and borrowing power, are of particular importance. Financial resources are essential only for a short time, but at the end of the stage of success, they lose their significance. In the stage of existence, survival, initial period of success, success, growth, and take-off, financial resources are included in the critical factors conditioning of the company. According to Churchill and Lewis (1983), the importance of cash changes as the business changes. It is a crucial resource at the start, becomes easily manageable at the success stage, and is the main concern again if the organisation begins to grow. As growth slows at the end of Stage IV or in Stage V, cash becomes a manageable factor again. The companies in Stage III need to recognise the financial needs and risk entailed in a move to Stage IV.

Churchill and Lewis's model concentrates mainly on the evolution of the organisation structure in the stages of a firm's growth.

Scott and Bruce (1987) develop a model of small business growth and try to isolate the main factors which will be important in each stage of growth and the type of crisis to be faced in moving from one stage to the next. There are five stages in this model. We describe the main features of each stage and, the most likely, crises briefly.

Stage I: Inception. The main efforts in this stage are developing a commercially acceptable product and establishing the place for it in the market. A high level of uncertainty characterises this stage. The main sources of financing in this stage are the founder's and his/her partner's savings, friends, and relatives. During this stage, the primary focus switches from the unit establishment and its product to the generation of positive cash flow or even a firm's profitability or losses' curbing. It requires formalisation of the system and record-keeping. If the firm is to survive, there is a need for changes in organisation structure and concentration of efforts on new aspects of the business.

Stage II: Survival. The main ways of business's growth are market expansion. The level of competition depends on the entry barriers existing in the industry and profitability. If the entry barriers are low, then the competition will increase. On the other hand, if profitability is relatively high and the businesses are attractive, the competition also will increase. In this stage, the financing emphasis swings to the working capital management and the need to finance increased inventories and receivables. The additional sources of finance are bank overdraft, short-term loans, and creditor financing if the firm has established credibility with its suppliers. The most likely crisis may occur because of overtrading or uncontrolled growth, increased complexity of expanded distribution channels, changes in the basis of competition, and pressures for information. If the firm is to grow, there is a need of new control systems, among which are cost and budgetary control system, the evolution of management system with the greater delegation, and new sources of financing for plant modernisation and expansion.

Stage III: Growth. In this stage, a firm is profitable with increased demand for working capital financing. The organisation structure is more formal, and the product range may be expanded in small scale due to the lack of resources available for the firm. The owners may sell the business at this stage with substantial capital gain. The main problem of the firm is liquidity. There are two primary sources of crisis in this stage. The first one is connected to the entry of larger competitors which may use economies of scale as a significant competitive weapon. It will result in pressure on price. The response is to forfeit market share and to compete on a differentiation basis exchanging volume for margin. To succeed this will require the investment of time and resources in product development. It practically means staying in Stage III. Alternatively, the firm can compete by implementing expansion into new markets or products. In this case, the key issue will be financing the growth and maintaining the control of operations. The challenge is to adapt the management style and introduce decentralisation.

Stage IV: Expansion. As in the previous stage, the long-term funds will be necessary during the firm's expansion. The major form of financing is retained earnings. The company's track record of successful operation will now allow it to seek long-term debt. But in this case, the firm will provide its assets as security. The successful firm's operation depends on the competitive environment. Owners could sell the firm at a reasonable price, but if the firm is not well managed, then it may drop back to the growth stage or even bankrupt. Which is the main crisis cause in this stage? The most likely crisis is the distance of top management from the action and the need for external focus, which means focus on customer needs and the product's adaptation.

Stage V: Maturity. In this stage, the company is still growing. Some of them may move out of being a small business. The key issues are expense control, productivity, innovativeness, and growth opportunities. In this stage, long-term debt may be necessary. The shareholder's pressure for ensuring the future of the company may be an important problem for the firm's managers.

La Rocca et al. (2011), analysing capital structure decisions during a firm's life cycle, concluded that in bank-oriented economies, firms tend to adopt specific financing strategies and a different hierarchy of financial decision-making as they progress through the phases of their life cycle. Berger and Udell (1998) suggest that the phase of a business' life cycle determines the nature of its financial needs, the availability of financial resources, and the related cost of capital. According to these authors, '(…) A small business may be thought of as having a financial growth cycle in which financial needs and options change as the business grows, gains further experience, and become less informationally opaque'. The brief description of basic life cycle theory for SMEs, which can be found earlier, makes it clear that the individual stages of a small business life are different concerning growth opportunities, the ability of cash generation, and risk connected with firm's operation. The model developed by Scott and Bruce (1987) is particularly characteristic. The sources of the crisis presented in it relate to the above factors, and mainly with the risk. All this affects the preferences and the possibility of choice as part of financial decisions taken in SMEs in individual phases of their lives. One can risk the hypothesis that the smaller the company, the higher the relative possibilities of its growth. If such an assumption can be verified, then the need for financing is also higher, and on the other hand, the opportunities of self-financing are limited. At the same time, companies in the early stages of their development are characterised by high information asymmetry and, therefore, have the most difficulty in obtaining intermediated external finance. On the other side, during the firm's growth, its balance sheet reflect increasing of tangible assets (buildings, equipment, inventory, accounts receivable) that might be pledged as collateral. Therefore, the availability of bank and commercial finance companies lending will be more available. But it will be to the disadvantage of innovative and high-risk companies. On the other side, many small business loans are personally guaranteed by the firm's owners. So, the possibilities of using lending, in this case, depending on the owner's wealth, creditworthiness, his reputation, his personality, and relationship with financing institutions. It shows that another factor is the legal status of a small business. During the life cycle, firms may accumulate retained earnings and increase the ability of self-financing.

Berger and Udell (1998) examine firm continuum and sources of finance using three main variables: firm size, firm age, and information availability. They distinguish four cases:

Case 1. Very small firms, possibly with no collateral and no track record.
Case 2. Small firms, possibly with high growth potential but often with a limited track record.

Case 3. Medium-sized firms with some track record, collateral available if necessary.
Case 4. Large firms of known risk and track record.

For each one of the above cases, they determine the possible sources of financing. They may be substitutes or complements:

Case 1. Initial insider finance (funds provided by the start-up team, family, and friends before and at the time of the firm's inception), angel finance, and trade credit. As the firm grows, it may gain access to the short- and intermediate-term financial institutions.
Case 2. Initial insider finance, venture capital, trade credit, short- and intermediate-term financial institutions, and mezzanine fund financing.
Case 3. Venture capital, trade credit, commercial papers, short- and intermediate-term financial institutions, medium-term notes, and private placements.
Case 4. Public equity, trade credit, commercial papers, short- and intermediate-term financial institutions, medium-term notes, private placements, and public debt.

The summary of this model is shown in Table 1.1.

Berger and Udell (1998) suggest that in the earlier stages, it will be difficult or even impossible to find external financing, and as a result, young and new firms will be less leveraged. There is another factor which should be

Table 1.1 Main sources of financing and a firm's financial growth cycle

	Smaller/younger/ opaquer firm	*Small firm*	*Medium-sized firm*	*Large firm*
Initial insider finance	X	X		
Angel finance	X			
Venture capital		X	X	
Public equity			X	X
Trade credit	X	X	X	X
Commercial paper				X
Short-term financial institution loans		X	X	
Intermediate-term financial institution loans		X	X	X
Medium-term notes			X	X
Mezzanine fund financing		X		
Private placements		X	X	
Public debt				X

Source: Udel and Berger (1998).

analysed. Firms using external funds need to service interest payments and as a result, shall have positive cash flow. Usually, it is difficult to achieve by many young companies.

Consequently, young firms use initial insider finance, angel finance, and during the later stages, they may use venture capital. Trade credit is vital in all stages. But the level of its use depends on age and reputation. As far as bank debt is considered, its use depends on the tangible assets owned by the firm and so is especially important for mature and less informationally opaque firms. As the firms mature, the creditworthiness increase and problems of moral hazard are reduced. In general, and as it was discussed before, the use of external sources of financing increases during the firm's life cycle.

Some researchers connect the availability of initial insider finance with the economic and demographic situation of the country. Worsening of the condition may influence a new firm's formation (Brewer et al., 1996).

Weston and Brigham (1970) present six phases of the financial life cycle. They connect each phase with the main available sources of financing and main financial problems characteristic for each stage. Access to sources of capital is determined, to a large extent, by the firm's development phase, which has a significant impact on the evaluation of its creditworthiness. During the early phases of their growth, firms must rely primarily on financial resources possessed by their owners and their families, sometimes on assistance funds or venture capital. During further phases of its development, the firm is financed primarily from the accumulation of financial surpluses and additionally using external capital. Mature firms (mainly medium-sized enterprises) have easier access to external capital and bank loans than other groups of firms from the SME sector (Table 1.2). External capital becomes the main source allowing to finance the firm's investment projects in the situation when internal accumulation capabilities of SMEs are limited. Insufficient availability of external capital can restrict the firm's growth opportunities. The main sources of external capital for SMEs are the so-called 'non-banking sources' of financing (trade credit, lease, factoring, franchising, loans from the non-banking sector) and bank loans (short and long terms). The SME sector also has access to capital provided by different types of assistance programmes and funds allocated in the framework of government projects assisting SMEs. In most countries, commercial banks are the primary source of finance for SMEs, so if the SME sector is to flourish, it must have access to bank credit (EOS Gallup Europe, 2005). Since SMEs (due to their size) are unable to raise investment capital in the capital market, the banking system becomes the only real opportunity of raising additional financial resources. This situation is theoretically advantageous for the SMEs due to the detailed evaluation of an investment project by the bank, which implies, among other things, the feasibility analysis of a project and professional counselling provided by the bank's employees. On the other hand, the position of SMEs in the bank loans market is determined by a strong influence exerted by structural characteristics of these enterprises.

Table 1.2 Financial life cycle of the firm

Phase	*Sources of finance*	*Main problems*
Inception	Owners' resources	Undercapitalization
Growth I	As above plus: Retained profits, trade credit, bank loans and overdrafts, hire purchase, leasing	Overtrading, liquidity crises
Growth II	As above plus: Longer term finance from financial institutions	Finance gap
Growth III	As above plus: New market issue	Loss of control
Maturity	All sources available	Maintaining ROI
Decline	Withdrawal of finance: Firm taken over, liquidation	Falling ROI

Source: Weston and Brigham (1970), p. 157; in C. Mac An Bhaird, *Resourcing Small and Medium Sized Enterprises, Contribution to Management Science*, Springer-Verlag: Berlin and Heidelberg, 2010.

As noted at the beginning of this part of the chapter, the life cycle models do not fit all businesses. When we try to connect the sources of financing and the decision of the firm's capital structure with the theory of the firm's life cycle, we note that there are some factors which are essential in this analysis. For example,

1. Industry affiliation. According to Harris and Raviv (1991), firms in the same industry sector have a similar ratio of leverage and different industries vary while leverage is examining. If so, then the industry sector is a significant determinant of the leverage ratio. Industry sector affects the level of tangible assets, business risk, growth opportunities, and as a result, the debt ratio (Porter, 1980; La Rocca et al., 2011).
2. Type of financial system: bank-based and market-based (this aspect is presented in Chapter 3).
3. The efficiency of the financial system. An efficient financial system is fundamental to supporting economic growth and a higher rate of productivity (Rajan and Zingales, 1995; Wald, 1999; Booth et al., 2002).
4. The institutional environment measured by a plethora of variables like bureaucratic and regulatory quality (Titman et al., 2003; Gaud et al., 2005).

Notes

1 The total risk associated with an action is composed of two elements: systemic risk, which is a portion of the total risk that attributes to the movement of the market as a whole, and unsystematic risk, which is the residual risk that is unique to a specific area. Systematic risk is attributable to the common economic factor, say overall economic conditions that affect all assets in the economy in a similar manner. Such factors would include the general level of demand in the marketplace, interest rates, inflation rates, and labour costs. This type of risk cannot be diversified through asset combinations. Unsystematic risk is unique

or distinctive to the individual asset. This type of risk can be almost eliminated through diversification. This kind of risk is also called specific risk. We can also classify total risk as follows: (1) Economic risk which reflects risks of the overall economic environment in which the enterprise operates, including general economic risk (fluctuations in business activity), capital market risk (including changes in interest rates), and purchasing power risk. (2) Business risk or operating risk is concerned with the ever-present uncertainty regarding a business enterprise's ability to earn a satisfactory return on its investments as well as with the multitude of cost and revenue factors of competition, product mix, changes in consumer preferences, prices of factor inputs, labour strikes, and management ability. (3) Financial risk is concerned with capital structure and with the ability of an enterprise to meet fixed charges and claims.

2 The potential costs of bankruptcy may be both direct and indirect. Examples of direct bankruptcy costs are the legal and administrative costs in the bankruptcy process. Examples of indirect bankruptcy costs are the loss in profits incurred by the firm as a result of the unwillingness of stakeholders to do business with them (Titman, 1984).

References

Abor, J., 2005, The effect of capital structure on profitability: An empirical analysis of listed firms in Ghana, *The Journal of Risk Finance*, Vol. 6, No. 5, pp. 438–445.

Aggarwal, R., Zong, S., 2006, The cash flow-investment relationship: International evidence of limited access to external finance, *Journal of Multinational Financial Management*, Vol. 16, No. 1, pp. 89–104.

Akerlof, G., 1970, The market for lemons: Quality uncertainty and the market mechanism, *The Quarterly Journal of Economics*, Vol. 84, No. 3, pp. 488–500.

Allen, W.A., Wood, G., 2006, Defining and achieving financial stability, *Journal of Financial Stability*, Vol. 2, No. 1, pp. 152–172.

Awan, H.W., Bhatti, M.I., Ali, R., Qureshi, A., 2010, How growth opportunities are related to corporate leverage decisions? *Investment Management and Financial Innovations*, Vol. 7, No. 1, pp. 90–97.

Baylis, J., Smith, S., Owens, P., 2014, *The Globalization of World Politics – An Introduction to International Relation*, Oxford University Press: Oxford.

Beck, T., Demirgüç-Kunt, A., Levine, R., 2009, *Financial Institutions and Markets across Countries and over Time*, Policy Research Working Paper No. 4943.

Berger, A.N., Udell, G.F., 1998, The economics of small business finance: The roles of private equity and debt markets in the financial growth cycle, *Journal of Banking and Finance*, Vol. 22, No. 6/8, pp. 613–673.

Booth, L., Aivazian, V. Demirguc-Kunt, A., Maksimovic, V., 2002, Capital structure in developing countries, *The Journal of Finance*, Vol. 56, No. 1, pp. 87–130.

Brewer, E., Genay, H., Jackson, W.E., Worthington, P.R., 1996, How are small firms financed? Evidence from small business investment companies, *Economic Perspectives*, Federal Reserve Bank of Chicago, issue Nov, pp. 2–18.

Chandler, A., 1962, *Strategy and Structure: Chapters in the History of Industrial Enterprise*, Doubleday: New York.

Chang, C.P., Lee, C.C., 2010, Globalization and economic growth: A political economy analysis for OECD countries, *Global Economic Review, Perspectives on East Asian Economies and Industries*, Vol. 39, No. 2, pp. 151–173.

Chant, J., 2003, Financial stability as a policy goal, in Chant, J., Lai, A., Illing, M., Daneil, F., *Essays on Financial Stability*, Technical Report No. 95, Bank of Canada, Ottawa.

Chen, L., Zhao, X., 2006, On the relation between the market-to-book ratio, growth opportunity, and leverage ratio, *Finance Research Letters*, Vol. 3, No. 4, pp. 253–266.

Churchill, N.C.; Lewis, V.L., 1983, The five stages of small business growth, *Harvard Business Review*, Vol. 61, No. 3, pp. 30–50.

Coase, R.H., 1937, The Nature of the Firm, *Economica*, Vol. 4, pp. 386–405.

Donaldson, G., 1961, *Corporate Debt Capacity: A Study of Corporate Debt Policy and the Determination of Corporate Debt Capacity*, Division of Research, Harvard School of Business Administration: Boston, MA.

EOS Gallup Europe, 2005, *Flash Eurobarometer – SMEs Access to Finance in the EU-15*, retrieved on 12/08/2018 from https://ec.europa.eu/growth/content/flash-eurobarometer-smes-access-finance-eu-15-0_pl

Fama, E., French, K., 2002, Testing trade-off and pecking order predictions about dividends and debt, *Review of Financial Studies*, Vol. 15, pp. 31–43.

Fazzari, S., Hubbard, R., Petersen, B., Blinder, A., Poterba, J., 1988, Financing constraints and corporate investment, *Brookings Papers on Economic Activity*, Vol. 1, No. 1, pp. 141–195.

Ferrari-Filho, F., Conceicao, O.A.C., 2005, The concept of uncertainty in post keynesian theory and institutional economics, *Journal of Economic Issues*, Vol. XXXIX, No. 3, September, pp. 107–137.

Frankel, J., 2000, *Globalization of the Economy*, Working Paper No. 7858, retrieved on 10/8/2018 from http://www.nber.org/papers/w7858.pdf

Fusari, A., 2016, *A New Economics for Modern Dynamic Economies*, MPRA Paper No. 74008, retrieved on 7/9/2018 from https://mpra.ub.uni-muenchen.de/74008/

Fusari, A., 2017, *A New Economics for Modern Dynamic Economies*, Routledge: London.

Gale, R., 2006, Environmental management accounting as a reflexive modernization strategy in cleaner production, *Journal of Clean Production*, Vol. 14, pp. 1228–1236.

Gaud, P., Jani, E., Hoesli, M., Bender, A., 2005, The capital structure of Swiss companies: An empirical analysis using dynamic panel data, *European Financial Management*, Vol. 11, No. 1, pp. 51–77.

Greenwald, B., Stiglitz, J., 1990, Asymmetric information and the new theory of the firm: Financial constraints and risk behaviour, *The American Economic Review*, Vol. 80, No. 2, pp. 160–165.

Greiner, L. 1972, Evolution and revolution as organisations grow, *Harvard Business Review*, Vol. 50, No. 3, pp. 37–46.

Hanks, S.H., 1990, The organization life cycle: Integrating content and process, *Journal of Small Business Strategy*, Vol. 1, No. 2, pp. 1–13.

Hanks, S.H. (ed.), 1993, Tightening the life-cycle construct: A taxonomic study of growth stage configurations in high-technology organisations, *Entrepreneurship: Theory and Practice*, Vol. 18, No. 2, pp. 5–30.

Harris, M., Raviv, A., 1991, The theory of capital structure, *The Journal of Finance*, Vol. 46, No. 1, pp. 297–355.

Hefferman, S., 2005, *Modern Banking*, John Wiley & Sons Ltd.

Hubbard, R.G., 1995, Is there a credit channel for monetary policy?, *Federal Reserve Bank of St. Louis Review*, Vol. 77, No. 3, pp. 63–77.

International Monetary Fund, retrieved on 06/05/2018 from http://www.imf.org/external/pubs/ft/gfsr/2007/01/pdf/
Jensen, M., 1986, Agency cost of free cash flow, corporate finance, and takeovers, *The American Economic Review*, Vol. 76, No. 2, pp. 323–329.
Jensen, M., Meckling, W., 1976, Theory of the firm: Managerial behaviour, agency costs, and capital structure, *Journal of Financial Economics*, Vol. 3, No. 4, pp. 305–360.
Kester, W.C., 1986, Capital and ownership structure: A comparison of the United States and Japanese manufacturing corporations, *Financial Management*, Vol. 15, pp. 5–16.
Kose, M.A., Prasad, E., Rogoff, K., Wei, S.J., 2007, Financial globalization: Beyond the blame game, *Finance & Development*, March, Vol. 44, No. 1, pp. 157–176.
La Rocca, M., La Rocca, T., Cariola, A., 2011, Capital structure decisions during a firm's life cycle, *Small Business Economy*, Vol. 37, pp. 107–130.
Lester, D.L., Parnell, J.A., 1999, A strategic interpretation of organisation life cycle, *Journal of Applied Management and Entrepreneurship*, Vol. 5, No. 1, pp. 14–32.
Lester, D.L., Parnell, J.A., Carraher, S., 2003, Organization life cycle: A five-stage empirical scale, *The International Journal of Organizational Analysis*, Vol. 11, No. 4, pp. 339–354.
López-Gracia, J., Sogorb-Mira, F., 2008, Testing trade-off and pecking order theories financing SMEs, *Small Business Economics*, Vol. 31, No. 2, pp. 117–136.
Lorraine, N.H.S., Collison, D.J., Power, D.M., 2004, An analysis of the stock market impact of environmental performance information, *Account Forum*, Vol. 28, pp. 7–26.
Mac an Bhaird, C., 2010, *Resourcing Small and Medium Sized Enterprises, Contribution to Management Science*, Springer-Verlag: Berlin and Heidelberg.
Michaelas, N., Chittenden, F., Poutziouris, P., 1999, Financial policy and capital structure choice in U.K. SMEs: Empirical evidence from company panel data, *Small Business Economics*, Vol. 2, No. 12, pp. 113–130.
Miller, M.H., 1977, Debt and taxes, *Journal of Finance*, Vol. 32, No. 2, May, pp. 261–275.
Mishkin, F., 1999, Global financial instability: Framework, events, issues, *Journal of Economic Perspectives*, Vol. 13, No. 4, pp. 3–20.
Modigliani, F., Miller, M.H., 1958, The cost of capital, corporate finance, and the theory of investment, *American Economic Review*, Vol. 48, No. 3, pp. 261–275.
Modigliani, F., Miller, M.H., 1963, Corporate income taxes and the cost of capital: A correction, *American Economic Review*, Vol. 53, No. 3, pp. 276–298.
Mundell, R., 1995, The international monetary system: The missing factor, *Journal of Policy Modelling*, Vol. 5, No. 17, pp. 479–492.
Myers, S.C., 1977, Determinants of corporate borrowing, *Journal of Financial Economics*, Vol. 9, pp. 147–176.
Myers, S.C., 1984, The capital structure puzzle, *Journal of Finance*, No. 39, pp. 575–592.
Myers, S.C., Majluf, N., 1984, Corporate financing and investment decisions when firms have information that investors do not have, *Journal of Financial Economics*, Vol. 13, No. 2, pp. 187–221.
Odagiri, H., 1994, *Growth through Competition, Competition through Growth*, Clarendon Press: Oxford.
O'Farrell, P.N., Hitchens, W.N., 1988, Alternative theories of small-firm growth: A critical review, *Environment, and Planning*, Vol. 20, pp. 1365–1383.

Pandey, I.M., 2001, *Capital Structure and the Firm Characteristics: Evidence from an Emerging Market*, IIMA Working Paper No. 2001-10-04.

Porter, M., 1980, *Competitive Strategies: Techniques for Analysing Industries and Competitors*, The Free Press: New York.

Queen, M., Roll, R., 1987, Firm mortality: Using market indicators to predict survival, *Financial Analysts Journal*, Vol. 43, No. 3, pp. 9–26.

Rajan, R.G., Zingales, L., 1995, What do we know about capital structure? Some evidence from international data, *Journal of Finance*, Vol. 50, pp. 1421–1460.

Romer, P.M., 1986, Increasing returns and long-run growth, *The Journal of Political Economy*, October, Vol. 94, No. 5, pp. 1002–1037.

Schinazi, G.J., 2004, *Defining Financial Stability*, International Monetary Fund, Working Paper No. 04/187.

Scott, M., Bruce, R., 1987, Five stages of growth in small business, *Long Range Planning*, Vol. 20, No. 3, pp. 45–52.

Smith, C., 1977, Alternative methods for raising capital: Rights versus underwritten offerings, *Journal of Financial Economics*, Vol. 5, pp. 273–307.

Stiglitz, J.E., 2001, *Information and the Change in the Paradigm in Economics*, Aula Magna Nobel Prize Lecture, December 8, by Columbia Business School, Columbia University Press.

Storey, D., 1994, *Understanding the Small Business Sector*, Routledge: London.

Titman, S., 1982, *Determinants of Capital Structure: An Empirical Analysis*, Working Paper, UCLA.

Titman, S., 1984, The effect of capital structure on a firm's liquidation decisions, *Journal of Financial Economics*, Vol. 13, pp. 137–151.

Titman, S., Fan, J., Twite, G., 2003, *An International Comparison of Capital Structure and Debt Maturity Choices*, Working Paper, University of Texas: Austin.

Titman, S., Wessels, R., 1988, The determinants of capital structure choice, *Journal of Finance*, Vol. XLIII, No. 1, pp. 51–71.

Wald, J.K., 1999, How firm characteristics affect capital structure: An international comparison, *Journal of Financial Research*, Vol. 22, No. 22, pp. 161–187.

Wang, C.A., 2008, Is its heavy log that broke the camel's back? Evidence of the credit channel in Taiwan's construction industry, *International Real Estate Review*, Vol. 11, No. 1, pp. 38–64.

Weston, J., Brigham, E., 1970, *Managerial Finance*, 3rd Edition, Holt, Rinehart and Winston: New York.

2 Small and medium enterprises in Greece

2.1 Introduction

The small and medium-sized enterprise (SME) sector is considered crucial to European competitive development. It employs the majority of the European labour force and commands two-thirds of sales volume in the non-primary sector. Small and medium enterprises also played a significant role in the economies of the Central and East European countries during the transition period. The importance of the SME sector in these economies was correlated with such reasons as demonopolisation of the economy, social stability through the development of the middle class, and creation of a significant number of new jobs.

In the last decade, SMEs are considered with an increasing interest by European policymakers, public authorities, and economists who are trying to support them in finding financial resources and establishing cooperative relationships to help them remain viable and competitive.

SMEs are a significant source of entrepreneurial skills, innovation, growth, and employment. Although there is a general belief that SMEs are essential for the economy of each country, there is no consensus on how to define them. Institutions, states, researchers, and even statistical agencies use different definitions of SMEs. In the determination of what is an SME, qualitative and quantitative criteria can be used or a combination of these two groups of criteria. Qualitative criteria allow distinguishing small and medium enterprises from large enterprises. They allow determining their characteristic features. Definition based on qualitative criteria may be used mainly in researches in the field of management and organisation. These criteria do not allow statistical analysis of these enterprises and cannot be used for the implementation of the support policies. Therefore, for those purposes, the quantitative criteria are generally used. The most commonly applied quantitative criteria are a number of employees, annual turnover, and the value of fixed assets. The definition of an SME used in this research is based on the employment criterion. It means that any enterprise with fewer than 250 employees is considered an SME.

Greece is often considered as a country of SMEs. The data available confirm the predominant role that SMEs play in the Greek economy, since they account for the larger share of both employment and total value added than the EU average. According to the data, all but 0.1 per cent of enterprises which operated in Greek non-financial business sector in 2016 were SMEs. SMEs contributed 73.2 per cent of the value added generated within the Greek economy and 86.9 per cent of total employment. Micro SMEs are by far the most common type of SMEs in Greece. More than 9.6 out of 10 (96.2 per cent) enterprises in Greece were microenterprises, with a share of employment within the non-financial business economy of 57.3 per cent. These figures are well above the EU average, especially in the services and trade sector. Due to this fact, the financial performance and viability of SMEs are fundamental to the Greek economy as well as to investors, bankers, and their suppliers. The processes of integration and globalisation have brought strong competition to the Greek SMEs sector. Their situation has worsened significantly during the recent crisis. At present, many of these enterprises face survival problems. One of the preconditions for firms' operation and growth in a competitive environment is the access to sources of financing. To be competitive, the firms must first be financially viable. Although the role of the Greek SMEs is vital to the Greek economy, the existing literature on this topic is rather limited.

This chapter attempts to provide answers to crucial questions such as which are the main quantitative and qualitative criteria used for SMEs definition, how SME is defined in different countries, organizations, and researchers, which is the current situation of SMEs in Greece, which is their structure and contribution to employment and economic activity in the European context, and, finally, which are the main constraints preventing Greek SMEs from growing and generating more jobs and economic growth during the period under investigation.

2.2 Defining small and medium enterprises: an overview

Defining an SME is not easy. In literature, a variety of definitions may be found, and a standard international definition of SME does not exist. Academics, authors, and policymakers apply SME definitions in terms of a dichotomy between universality and standardisation of a unique definition and relativity and sectored specialisation (Berisha and Pula, 2015). Analysing the problem in two main dimensions, it should be noted that:

1 As the scale of business activity increases over time, the definition of SME changes.
2 In various countries and groups of countries (e.g. in the USA and the EU), statistical agencies and institutions with different criteria for determining enterprises regarding their size are used.

Storey (1994) discusses the problem of defining small firms and tries to sum up the danger of using size to determine the status of a firm. He concludes that no matter how they are defined, they constitute at least 95 per cent of businesses in the European Community. Storey tries to emphasise the importance of these enterprises for the economy and the need to intensify research on these enterprises. Without diminishing the claims proposed by this author, the problem should also be viewed from a different point of view. Intensification of research on SMEs requires a strict definition of the subject of study. Defining a small business is necessary to avoid misunderstanding the term. A definition is also an essential tool for determining and implementing efficiency measures, programmes, and policies to support the development and success of SMEs. According to Berisha and Pula (2015), the existence of different definitions at the national level could create inconsistencies. The same authors ask: 'If economists claim that small and medium enterprises are the backbone of the economy, they must be able to determine the number of them in the order of the discussions'.

Analysing companies that are not in the category of large enterprises, we can note that at international and national levels, some refers to them as small businesses, others use the term SMEs, while some others use the distinction on micro, small and medium enterprises. Abbreviation SME is usually used in the EU and international organisations like the World Bank, United Nations, and the World Trade Organization.

Although definitions of small business vary, they are all based on one or more of the quantitative and qualitative criteria (EC, 2007). The examples of quantitative criteria are the number of employees, the annual revenue, and the value of fixed assets.

The most commonly used qualitative criteria include decision-making independence, owner's liability for the company's obligations, the strong influence of the entrepreneur's personality on the functioning of the enterprise, organizational structure – SMEs have a transparent and straightforward organizational structure and a faster and more efficient information flow process, ownership (e.g. whether the business is independently owned).

It is also possible to use mixed criteria, which arises from the combination of quantitative and qualitative criteria. It considers, among others, relatively small market share, direct management of the company by the owners, and labour-intensive method of production.

The use of quantitative and qualitative criteria aimed at distinguishing SMEs from the whole economy may have significant practical utility and meet the specific needs of economic policy, thanks to the fact that it will contribute to:

- The formulation and implementation of an effective policy to promote and support the development of the SME sector.
- The building an effective system of financing the development of SMEs, including the tax system on the one hand and the external financing system on the other.
- Creating clear and easily comparable statistics allowing socio-economic analysis and surveys of the sector at the national as well as the international level.

When talking about small business, companies that are generally considered are those which meet the following conditions:

1 They have a small capital and employ a small number of employees.
2 They have a small market share and often the owner is a manager.
3 They are independent of other business entities.

Let us try to analyse some definitions used by organisations in different countries and most commonly used in the literature.

The Committee for Economic Development defines as small any business that satisfies any two of the following criteria (Committee for Economic Development, 1947):

1 Management is independent. Usually, the managers are also owners.
2 Capital is supplied and an individual or a small group hold ownership.
3 Area of operations is mainly local. Workers and owners are in one home community, but markets need not be local.
4 Relatively small size within the industry.

Bolton Committee in its 1971 'Report on Small Firms' (Bolton, 1971) descript the critical characteristics of a small firm. This stated that a small firm meets the following three criteria:

1 It is an independent business and not forming part of a large enterprise.
2 It is managed by its owners and not through a formalised management structure.
3 It is having a relatively small market share.

The Bolton Report also adopted a number of different statistical definitions (Bolton, 1971). It recognised that size is relevant to the sector. For example, a firm of a given size could be small concerning one sector where the market is large and there are many competitors, whereas a firm of similar proportions could be considered large in another sector with fewer players and generally smaller firms within it. Similarly, it recognised that it might be more appropriate to define size by the number of employees in some sectors but more appropriate to use turnover in others. Whereas firms in manufacturing, construction, and mining were defined in terms of number of employees (in which case, 200 or less qualified the firm to be a small firm), those in the wholesale trades, motor trades, retailing, and miscellaneous services were defined in terms of turnover (in which case the range is £50,000–£200,000 or less to be classified as small firm). Firms in the road transport industry are classified as small if they have five or fewer vehicles (Bolton, 1971; Abor and Quartey, 2010).

As mentioned earlier, the small business group is not homogenous and many definitions make a distinction between micro, small, and medium-sized enterprises.

The Companies Act of 1985 (Section 248) states that a company is 'small' if it satisfies at least two of the following criteria:

- A turnover of not more than £2.8 million.
- A balance sheet total of not more than £1.4 million.
- Not more than 50 employees.

A medium-sized company must satisfy at least two of the following criteria:

- A turnover of not more than £11.2 million.
- A balance sheet total of not more than £5.6 million.
- Not more than 250 employees.

For statistical purposes, the Department of Trade and Industry used the following definitions (Department of Trade and Industry, 2000a, 2000b):

- Micro firm: 0–9 employees
- Small firm: 0–49 employees (includes micro)
- Medium firm: 50–249 employees
- Large firm: over 250 employees

In North America, according to the Small Business Act (SBA), a small business concerns a business that is independently owned and operated and which is not dominant in its field of operation and conformity with specific industry criteria (SBA, 2013). SBA defines industry-specific size standards based on the average number of employees over the past 12 months or average annual receipts over the past 3 years categorised using the North American Industry Classification System (NAICS) codes. The definition is detailed and complex. It occupies 37 pages of SBA regulations. For example, in the construction industry, a business is defined as small if its average annual receipts for its preceding three fiscal years do not exceed $12 million, in retail industry the cut-off point for department stores is an annual sale which should not exceed $7.5 million, and in variety stores $2.5 million; in manufacturing, the primary criterion is the number of employees. In general, most manufacturing companies with 1,000 employees or fewer and most non-manufacturing businesses with average annual receipts under $12 million are qualified as small businesses. In the SBA of July 30, 1953, Congress created the Small Business Administration, an independent agency in the US government, whose function is to help preserve free and competitive enterprise in the economy. The agency is engaged in a variety of activities, including financing, procurement, and management assistance. Firms to be eligible for government contracts reserved for small businesses must meet size requirements set by the SBA. In practice, schemes which are nominally targeted at small firms adopt a variety of working definition depending on their particular objectives.

The World Bank uses three quantitative criteria for defining SMEs: number of employees, total assets in US dollars, and annual sales in US dollars.

According to the World Bank standards, a business must meet the quantitative criteria of a number of employees and at least one financial criterion to be categorised as micro, small, or medium business (Independent Evaluation Group, 2008). The number of employees by the enterprise size is as follows:

- Micro: no more than ten employees.
- Small: no more than 50 employees.
- Medium: no more than 300 employees.

Financial criteria by the enterprise size are as follows:

- Micro: total assets below \$100,000 or total annual sales below \$100,000.
- Small: total assets >\$100,000 and ≤\$3,000,000 or total annual sales >\$100,000 and ≤\$3,000,000.
- Medium: total assets >\$3,000,000 and ≤\$15,000,000 or total annual sales >\$3,000,000 and ≤\$15,000,000.

According to the Industrial Development Organization of the United Nations (UNIDO), there is no formal and generally accepted definition for SMEs, which are categorised differently from country to country and within countries, depending on the objectives of various regulatory and incentive systems. In a functional approach, UNIDO defines SMEs as enterprises that are too small to achieve an optimal division of labour, and thus an internal specialisation in their business operations (UNIDO, 1999). The Industrial Development Organization of the United Nations also defines SMEs concerning a number of employees by giving different classifications for industrialised and developing countries (UNIDO, 2004). The definition for industrialised countries is given as follows:

- Large – firms with 500 or more workers.
- Medium – firms with 100–499 workers.
- Small – firms with 99 or fewer workers.

The classification given for developing countries is as follows:

- Large – firms with 100 or more workers.
- Medium – firms with 20–99 workers.
- Small – firms with 5–19 workers.
- Micro – firms with less than five workers.

It also describes the qualitative indicators in discerning SMEs from large companies (UNIDO, 2004; Abor and Quartey, 2010; Berisha and Pula, 2015). SMEs are characterised by:

1. Management: proprietor – entrepreneurship, functions linked to personalities.
2. Personnel: lack of university graduates, all-around knowledge.
3. Organisation: highly personalised contacts.

4 Buyer's relationships: unstable.
5 Production: labour intensive.
6 Research development: following the market, intuitive approach.
7 Finance: the role of family funds, self-financing.

At the request of Council of Industry, the European Commission, an executive body of the European Union, proposed in February 1996 a first common SME definition. It was a recommendation that marked the beginnings of a unique definition of SMEs in the EU (European Commission, 1996). It was based on the idea that in a single market with no internal frontiers, it is essential that measures in favour of SMEs are based on a standard definition to improve their consistency and effectiveness and to limit distortions of competition. This is all the more necessary given the extensive interaction between national and EU measures to help SMEs in areas such as regional development and research funding. This definition has been widely applied throughout the EU. To qualify as an SME, both the employee and the independence criteria must be satisfied and either the turnover or the balance sheet total criteria (Table 2.1). The communication also includes a (non-binding) recommendation to the Member States, the European Investment Bank, and the European Investment Fund encouraging them to adopt the same definitions for their programmes. The communication permits them to use lower threshold figures if desired.

On May 6, 2003, the Commission adopted a new recommendation to take account of economic developments since 1996 like developments in prices and productivity (European Commission, 2003, 2005). The new SME definition was entered into force on January 1, 2005. According to the regulation of the European Commission, staff headcount and financial thresholds determine enterprise categories (European Commission, 2014). According to the Article 2 of the Annex of Recommendation 2003/361/EC,

> The category of micro, small and medium-sized enterprises (SMEs) is made up of enterprises which employ fewer than 250 persons and which have an annual turnover not exceeding 50 million euro, and/or an annual balance sheet total not exceeding 43 million euro.

Table 2.1 Definition of SMEs, European Commission, 1996

Criterion	*Micro*	*Small*	*Medium*
Maximum number of employees	9	49	249
Maximum annual turnover	–	€ 7 million	€ 40 million
Maximum annual balance sheet total	–	€ 5 million	€ 27 million
Maximum percentage owned by one or jointly by several enterprise(s) not satisfying the same criteria	–	25 per cent	25 per cent

Source: European Commission (1996).

The new definition provides for an increase in the financial ceilings: the turnover of medium-sized enterprises (50–249 employees) should not exceed € 50 million; that of small enterprises (10–49 employees) should not exceed € 10 million, while that of micro firms (less than 10 employees) should not exceed € 2 million. Alternatively, balance sheets for medium, small, and microenterprises should not exceed € 43 million, € 10 million, and € 2 million, respectively.

It is necessary to note that while it is compulsory to respect the staff headcount thresholds, an SME may choose to meet either the turnover or balance sheet ceiling. It does not need to satisfy both and may exceed one of them without losing its status. The new definition offers this choice since, by their nature, enterprises in the trade and distribution sectors have higher turnover figures than those in manufacturing. Providing an option between this criterion and the balance sheet total, which reflects the overall wealth of an enterprise, ensures that SMEs engaged in different types of economic activity are treated fairly.

Primary criteria for the qualification of the enterprise to the category of SMEs are (Table 2.2):

1 The category of micro, small and medium-sized enterprises is made up of enterprises which employ fewer than 250 persons and which have an annual turnover not exceeding € 50 million and/or an annual balance sheet total not exceeding € 43 million.
2 Within the SME category, a small enterprise is defined as an enterprise which employs fewer than 50 persons and whose annual turnover and/or annual balance sheet total does not exceed € 10 million.
3 Within the SME category, a microenterprise is defined as an enterprise which employs fewer than ten persons and whose annual turnover and/or annual balance sheet total does not exceed € 2 million.

These definitions are relevant when assessing which enterprises may benefit from EU funding programmes aimed at promoting SMEs as well as

Table 2.2 Definition of SMEs, European Commission, 2003

Criterion	*Micro*	*Small*	*Medium*
Maximum number of employees	<10	<50	<250
Maximum annual turnover	≤€ 2 million (previously not defined)	≤€ 10 million (in 1996 ≤€ 7 million)	≤€ 50 million (in 1996 ≤€ 40 million)
Maximum annual balance sheet total	≤€ 2 million (previously not defined)	≤€ 10 million (in 1996 ≤€ 5 million)	≤€ 43 million (in 1996 ≤€ 27 million)

Source: European Commission (2003).

concerning specific policies such as SME-specific competition rules. The European Commission policy concerning SMEs is mainly concentrated in five priority areas: the promotion of entrepreneurship and skills, the improvement of SMEs' access to markets, cutting red tape, the improvement of SMEs' growth potential, and strengthening dialogue and consultation with SME stakeholders.

In Structural Business Statistics (SBS), a database maintained by Eurostat, a primary source of data for an analysis of SMEs in the EU, mainly use the employment definition. The main classes used for presenting the results are (Eurostat, 2018):

- Microenterprises: with less than ten persons employed.
- Small enterprises: with 10–49 persons employed.
- Medium-sized enterprises: with 50–249 persons employed.
- SMEs: with 1–249 persons employed.
- Large enterprises: with 250 or more persons employed.

Only a limited set of the standard SBS variables (number of enterprises, turnover, persons employed, value added, etc.) is available mostly down to the three-digit (group) level of the activity classification (NACE), based on criteria that relate to the number of persons employed in each enterprise.

It is clear from the various definitions that there is no consensus over what constitutes an SME. From this analysis, we can conclude:

1 SMEs are companies without subsidiaries, independent, with a small number of employees.
2 The most common criterion to distinguish between large and small business is the number of employees. The number of employees varies from one country to another, the upper limit being 250 employees in the case of the EU. But others have adjusted the limit to 200 employees, while the UScompanies have less than 500 employees.
3 Financial criteria which are used in the SME definition differ between countries, organisations, and industries (annual turnover, balance sheet total, total assets, total annual sales, etc.).
4 Since there are differences in denomination, exchange rates make comparisons between countries difficult.
5 Since financial reporting standards vary between countries, comparisons between countries may be difficult.
6 Since the qualitative indicators are not easy to operationalise for statistical purposes and policies' implementation, quantitative criteria are usually used.

The data in the present research are based on the definition used by the SBS database of Eurostat. It means that unless otherwise specified, this research is based only on the employment definition and any enterprise with fewer than

250 employees are considered as a SME. The main groups used in this research are microenterprises with less than 10 persons employed, small enterprises with 10–49 persons employed, medium-sized enterprises with 50–249 persons employed, and large enterprises with 250 or more persons employed. This includes all types of enterprises, irrespective of their legal forms, such as family enterprises, sole proprietorships, or cooperatives. Despite the imperfection of this definition, it is used because of statistical usefulness, and in consequence the possibility of analysing and comparing its performance in Greece and other countries of the EU. For the sake of readability, the research uses the term SME throughout, unless a differentiation of sub-segments is needed.

2.3 Importance of SMEs and its main features

The most important measures of the role played by SMEs in the economy are the share of this sector in the total number of economic units, its share in total employment and gross value added, and its ability to create new jobs (OECD, 2010). According to Acs et al. (1999), the best measure of the relative importance of small business in the economy is a share of value added. According to the same authors, sales tend to underestimate the importance of small businesses and employment tends to overestimate the importance of small businesses because they are more labour-intensive than large companies.

The SMEs sector comprises the vast majority of firms in many economies regarding absolute numbers. In the European Union over, 99 per cent of businesses are classified as small and medium-sized enterprises. The SME sector is practically the only sector of the economy in contemporary developed countries, which generates net jobs. New job creation takes place both by setting up new economic units and through developing already operating firms (OECD, 2005). The SME sector is also a significant source of inventions (OECD, 1995). It distinguishes itself by high efficiency in the field of innovations launching them at lower costs than big companies. The importance of innovation propensity in the SME sector is emphasised more strongly in developed countries (Acs and Audretsch, 1987, Acs and Audretsch, 1991). Small innovative firms and especially those operating in high technology fields contribute significantly to creating and developing new fields of manufacturing, new industrial branches based on modern technologies. Small innovative firms are frequently fast-growing firms creating new jobs (Mulhern, 1995). Policymakers around the world continue trying to identify and support those productive, innovative small businesses that will generate employment and promote economic growth (Audretsch, 2004; Dobbs and Hamilton, 2007, International Labour Office, 2015). They shall encourage competition concerning price, product design and efficiency (Johnson and Soenen, 2003). The sustained growth of these businesses creates the new jobs and other benefits that communities are seeking while, at the same time, holding out to their owners the possibility of wealth, variety, self-fulfilment, and independence (Dobbs and Hamilton, 2007). Small enterprises often represent for persons their first step in the world of entrepreneurs. SMEs are more labour-intensive and tend to lead to a more equitable distribution of income than larger enterprises. They contribute to a more efficient allocation of resources and help to absorb productive resources at all levels of the economy and support the development and diffusion of entrepreneurial spirit and skills.

Characteristic is the role of SMEs in countries of former central planning economies. The establishment of broad ownership through the development of independent commercial enterprises, a good number of which are SMEs, creates the social basis for a competitive economic system. SMEs, moreover, are absorbing a considerable proportion of the labour force released by state firms in their adaptation to the new economic system. The creation of a healthy SME culture also helps to work against the distorted firm size structure typical of central planning, a structure characterised by a dominance of large firms and allocation decisions made by central authorities. This is even more remarkable given that SMEs, in comparison to privatised large firms and state enterprises, cannot usually rely on the helping hand of the state. SMEs are the most critical potential solution for labour market problems as progress in the macroeconomic restructuring of large former state firms continues. SMEs act as manufactures in production networks where they produce intermediate and final goods for market niches that increase the flexibility and efficiency of overall production.

Furthermore, SMEs act as distributors and wholesalers in internal and external trade. In this context, it is important to emphasise that SMEs link the larger firms to each other and the final consumer.

Moreover, SMEs ensures a competitive climate. Examples of the beneficial influence of small and medium-sized companies on the whole economy could be multiplied, but in general terms, the most important seems to be:

- They generate new jobs usually using relatively labour-intensive technologies.
- They generate innovations.
- They create ideas for new products and services.
- They efficiently and effectively fill existing market gaps unattractive for large companies.
- They contribute to the more effective allocation of market resources.

Economic theory suggests that SMEs differ significantly from large firms because SMEs have lower productivity and higher production costs due to small-scale production. Furthermore, they face higher supply cost and shorter supply terms, while they are forced to give longer credit terms to their customers as a means of sales promotion. SMEs sell mostly to final customers and operate in more segmented product markets. It is the larger firms that are more likely to export. The smaller firms depend more on their local economies than do large firms. This results in lower profitability and increased needs in working capital financing (Dunlop, 1992; Cosh and Hughes, 1993; Chittenden et al., 1996). The lack of adequate collateral, lack of information, low credibility, and higher financing costs coupled with SMEs' reluctance to issue capital, fearing loss of control of the firm, have resulted in lower use of long-term debt and high reliance on short-term financing (Gupta, 1969; Tamari, 1980; Ang, 1992; Chung, 1993). Some of those factors are of particular importance for SMEs since these firms are too small to have all the necessary resources ordinarily available in large enterprises (for reviews see: Acs, 1996; Acs et al., 1988, 1991). SMEs have fewer financial resources for innovation and fewer technological assets; they cannot create multidisciplinary research teams, they do not have access to 'global resources', knowledge, and so on (for reviews, see: Acs and Audretsch, 1987; Vanhaverbeke, 2011; Chesbrough, 2006). To survive, they have to cooperate with other firms and institutions (Hyz and Gikas, 2006; Hyz, 2010). Cooperation through the network helps them overcome some of those weaknesses (for reviews, see: Baum and Calabrese, 2000; Lee et al., 2010). They also suffer from many real disadvantages, for example, inability to spread risk over a portfolio of new products, difficulties in market start-up abroad, and problems in funding longer-term R&D (Rothwell and Dodgson, 1991). The individual characteristics of SMEs differ significantly. Each of the companies has its specific strategy (Barney, 1991) and 'way of behaviour' – from simple imitation to radical innovation. This influences SMEs demand for various types of external services (technical, advisory, financial, etc.) and contacts with the environment (other companies, R&D, supporting institutions, etc.).

Analysing the sector of SMEs using the SWOT analysis, we draw the following conclusions.

Main strengths:

- Strong business dynamics (especially a high birth rate).
- An increasingly higher level of education among its entrepreneurs.
- Increasing internationalisation of trade.
- High job-creating potential resulting from high birth rates and lower-than-average wages.
- The ability to quickly change the type of activity.
- Significant dynamism and rapid development.
- Strong motivation to work for both employees and employers.
- Ability to learn quickly.
- Successful in niche strategies.

Its weaknesses include:

- A high death rate, though usually lower than the birth rate.
- Lack of strategic marketing approaches and the custom of operating in highly segmented markets.
- low labour productivity resulting in high unit wage costs despite lower-than-average wages.
- The weak financial situation resulting from a low equity/debt ratio and costly loans.

- Price competitiveness.
- Low economic potential.
- The predominance of microenterprises.
- Concentration on the local market and low export ability.
- Low level of cooperation between enterprises.
- Lack of entrepreneurs' experience.
- Low level of knowledge about management and marketing.
- No strategy of action, focus on current operations.
- Low level of investment.
- Not recognising the intellectual capital of employees.

There are also some opportunities and threats in small and medium-sized sector development. More common opportunities are:

- Growing demand for personalised goods and services.
- Policies in the field of supporting entrepreneurship development and sustainable development of enterprises.
- Programmes for the use of special funds.
- International environment as a source of drawing resources, good practices in running a business.
- Broad access to new technologies.
- Easier doing business.
- Easier access to financing for launching and developing SME activities.

Among the main barriers or threats, the most important are:

- High volatility in the economy.
- Crisis phenomena, stagnation of the economy.
- Strong competition pressure.
- Economic slowdown.
- Costs of obtaining external financing sources.
- Difficulties in finding new markets.
- Cumbersome and lengthy administrative procedures.
- Required ways to secure the return of loan capital.
- The low social prestige of the entrepreneur.

2.4 Key indicators for enterprises in the non-financial business economy in Greece

SMEs are of great importance to the Greek non-financial business economy. Table 2.3 summarises the economic structure and contrasts the relative importance of SMEs with the EU-28 average for the year 2016. The data cover the non-financial business economy, which includes industry, construction, trade, and services (NACE Rev. 2 sections B to J, L, M, and N), but not enterprises in agriculture, forestry, and fisheries and the largely non-market service sectors such as education and health.

Table 2.3 The size and structure of the non-financial business economy, Greece and EU, 2016

Class size	*Number of enterprises*			*Number of persons employed*			*Value added*		
	Greece		*EU*	*Greece*		*EU*	*Greece*		*EU*
	Number	*Share %*	*Share %*	*Number*	*Share %*	*Share %*	*Billion €*	*Share %*	*Share %*
Micro	678,816	96.2	93	1,288,988	57,3	29.8	17	34.3	20.9
Small	23,829	3.4	5.8	412,490	18.3	20	9.5	19.2	17.8
Medium-sized	2,684	0.4	0.9	254,639	11.3	16.7	9.8	19.7	18.2
SMEs	705,329	99.9	99.8	1,956,117	86.9	66.6	36.3	73.2	56.8
Large	388	0.1	0.2	294,094	13.1	33.4	13.3	26.8	43.2
Total	705,717	100	100	2,250,211	100	100	49.6	100	100

Source: European Commission, SME Performance Review, 2018, https://ec.europa.eu/growth/smes/business-friendly-environment/performance-review_en

Considering the number of enterprises, SMEs account for 99.9 per cent of the total number of enterprises (Eurostat, 2017). This share is comparable to the EU average. Due to a high overall number of businesses, Greece is only slightly above average in terms of the proportion of SMEs as compared to all enterprises. According to the data for the Greek economy, there are approximately 66 SMEs per 1,000 inhabitants in Greece, which is significantly above the EU-27 average of ca 40 (EC, 2018). However, considering other indicators such as a share in employment and the creation of value added, it is easy to notice that their importance in the Greek economy is incomparably more significant than in other EU countries. About 87 per cent of the Greek workforce was active in an SME in 2016. The corresponding share in the countries of the EU is 66.6 per cent. The contribution of SMEs to employment in Greece is the highest among all member states of the EU. On average, Greek SMEs employ 2.8 persons against the EU average of around 3.9. The contribution of SMEs to total value added was lower than their contribution to total employment, resulting in a lower level of apparent labour productivity. Greek SMEs generate 73.2 per cent of total value added compared to 56.8 per cent in EU-28 (Figures 2.1 and 2.2). Greek SMEs productivity, measured as value added per the number of persons employed, is less than half the EU average (EC, 2018).

Very small enterprises, so-called 'microenterprises' dominate the Greek economy. This applies not only to the number but also to their share in employment and value-added creation. The small size of Greek SMEs is due to their strong domestic market orientation and small market size, in general, the low GDP per capita and the tendency to the self-employment. It is worth noting that the Mediterranean countries (Italy, Spain, Greece, Portugal, and southern France) have a greater preponderance of smaller firms than the generally wealthier northern European countries. The further north one goes in Europe, the larger average firm size tends to become. Denmark, Germany, France, and Britain, for example, have an average enterprise size over double that of Portugal, Spain, Italy, and Greece. Micro firms account

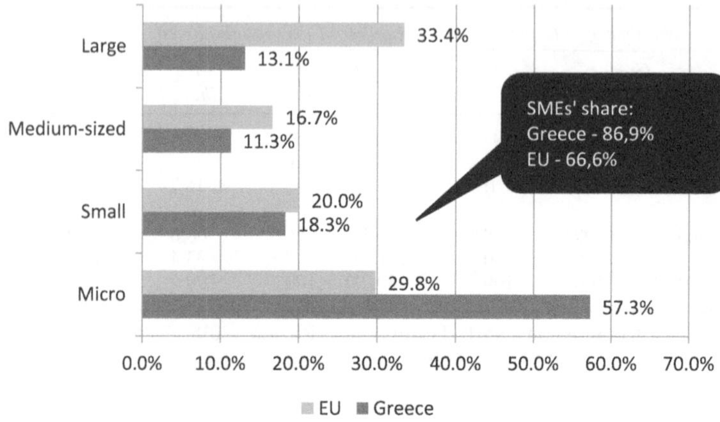

Figure 2.1 Contribution of different enterprise size categories to employment, Greece and EU, 2016.
Source: EC (2018).

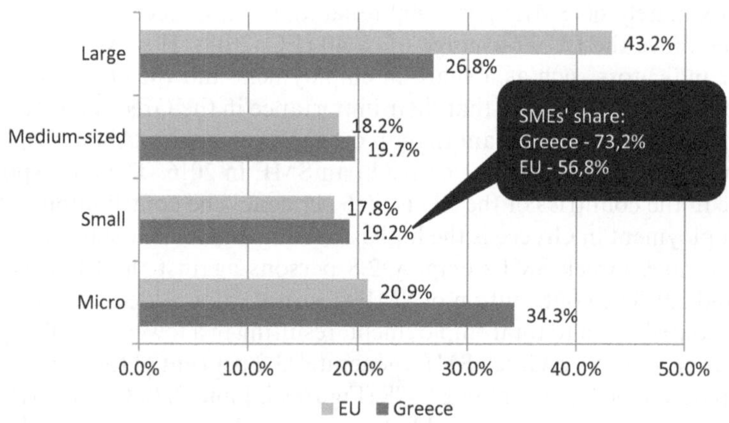

Figure 2.2 Contribution of different enterprise size categories to value added generated, Greece and EU, 2016.
Source: EC (2018).

in Greece for 96.2 per cent of the total number of SMEs (93 per cent in EU). Microenterprises employed more people than any other enterprises. Their share in employment is almost double in comparison to the EU average (57.3 per cent in Greece, 29.8 per cent EU average). The average employment size of micro firms in Greece in 2016 was 1.9 persons. This firm's size generates 34.3 per cent of total value added compared to the EU average of 20.9 per cent. According to the data for 2016, there are about 6,788,000 microenterprises, employing approximately 1.29 million people.

There are no significant differences between Greece and the EU as far as small firms are considered. Small firms accounted in 2016 for 18.3 per cent of total employment and 19.2 per cent of total value added in the Greek non-financial business sector. The contribution to employment and value added to this group of SMEs in EU member states is 20.0 per cent and 17.8 per cent, respectively. There are currently less than 24,000 small companies in Greece. They account for 3.4 per cent of the Greek non-financial business sector. Small enterprises have the smallest share in creating places work in the enterprise sector; they generate 18.3 per cent of jobs (number of employees in such companies is approximately 4,125,000 people). In an average small company, 21 people work.

The share of medium-sized companies in Greece in the total number of enterprises is significantly lower than the average in the EU (0.4 per cent and 0.9 per cent, respectively). Their share of employment in the case of Greece in 2016 was 11.3 per cent compared to 16.7 per cent in the EU and the share of value-added creation 19.7 per cent compared to 18.2 per cent in the EU member states. In 2016, there were about 27,000 medium-sized firms with about 255,000 people working in them.

There are currently 388 large companies in Greece, which represent 0.1 per cent of the Greek business sector. Currently, they are 10 per cent less than in 2008. Their participation in creating jobs is almost three times lower than the average in the EU. In the enterprise sector, they generate 13.1 per cent of jobs (the number of employees in such companies is around 295,000 people). Despite the small number of large companies, they have a relatively significant share in GDP at 26.8 per cent, although significantly lower than in the EU at 43.2 per cent. The share of large entities in generating GDP slightly decreased (from 2008 to 2016, it fell by 0.6 per cent). Comparing the current size structure of the Greek business economy with the EU average or other southern European countries, the business economy in Greece remains highly fragmented (Kritikos et al., 2018). Only 13.1 per cent of the workforce is employed in large firms. The share of employees in micro firms remains at a high level of 57.3 per cent.

Analysing the structure of the Greek economy, one should ask the question: to what extent does Greece has a balanced economic structure? Each economy, to function and develop, needs a diverse subjective structure. This structure is changing dynamically as the economic development progresses. In developed countries, SMEs as well as large enterprises have their place on the market. Each enterprise plays a specific role in the economic environment. It satisfies particular individual or collective needs, develops specific skills and technologies, provides employment, and more. In economies with a high degree of development, the core is large companies. In their environment, a creative sector of SMEs is developing, which responds quickly to market signals. As analysed in Section 2.3, these companies create cooperative relations with large enterprises. As a rule, the potential of SMEs is too low for them to conduct independent research on new technologies and new products. They base their innovative activity on the external acquisition of new technological solutions and patents. Often, the creation and development of small businesses are based on outsourcing or filling gaps existing on the market. There is no doubt that SMEs have a very important role to play, especially in the service or trade sector. It is doubtful that, however, for the author of this study, the possibility of development in sectors in which, for example, there is an effect of the scale of production. This conclusion seems all the more justified when we consider the geographical location of Greece, which is geographically distant from developed markets, and transport costs still play a vital role.

2.4.1 Distribution of firm size across industry sectors

Almost every second SME in Greece operates in the services sector and every third in the trade. The services sector was the largest in terms of value added and had the largest share in employment. Services activities accounted for 42.9 per cent of the SME population in the Greek non-financial sector (Table 2.4 and Figure 2.3). Their share in the number of persons employed in 2016 was 41.0 per cent and value-added creation 37.4 per cent. About 15 per cent were classified as professional, scientific, and technical activities, close to one in seven (13.5 per cent) were in accommodation and food services, and 9.1 per cent were in transportation and storage.

The trade sector operates 36.3 per cent of the total number of SMEs. In 2016, their share in employment and value-added creation was 36.5 per cent and 34.2 per cent, respectively.

The share of the two other sectors is lower. SMEs operating in the construction sector constitute 12.2 per cent of the total number of SMEs, and their share in employment and the creation of value added is 9.7 per cent and 9.1 per cent, respectively. The smallest number of enterprises operates in the

Table 2.4 SMEs indicators by the sector, Greece and EU, 2016

	Number of SMEs (%)		*Number of persons employed (%)*		*Value added (%)*	
	Greece	*EU*	*Greece*	*EU*	*Greece*	*EU*
Services	42.9	49	41	42.4	37.4	44.6
Trade	36.3	27	36.5	25.3	34.2	21.6
Construction	12.2	14.4	9.7	12	9.1	10.9
Manufacturing	8.5	8.9	12	19	17.6	19.7
Other	0.1	0.7	0.8	1.3	1.7	3.2

Source: EC (2018).

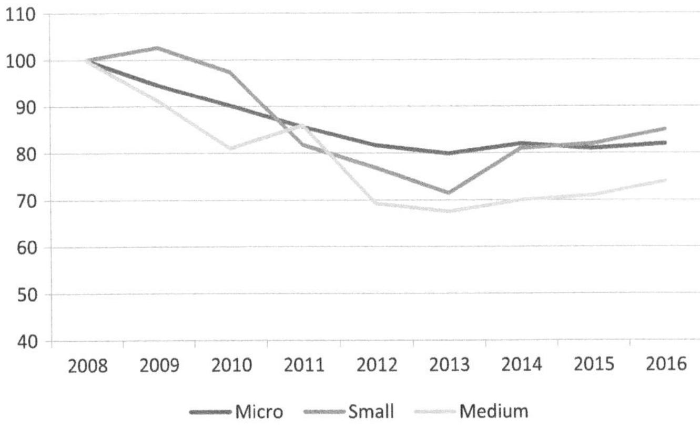

Figure 2.5 Number of persons employed in SMEs, Greece, 2008–2016.
Source: Own calculation based on EC (2016).

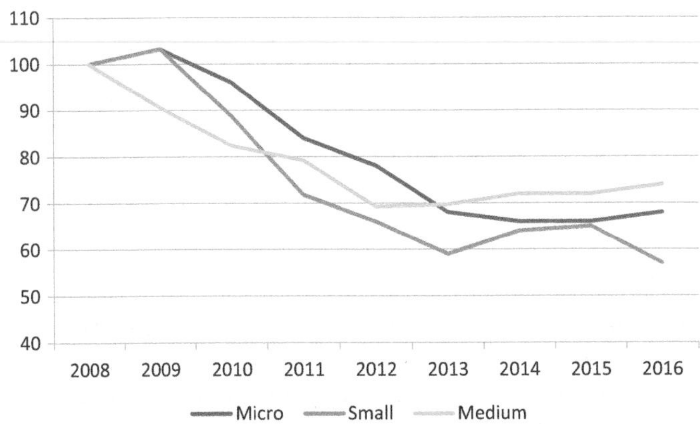

Figure 2.6 Value added of SMEs by size class, Greece, 2008–2016.
Source: Own calculation based on EC (2016).

Some results from the analysis show that the situation in the Greek small and medium-sized sector is far away from the Schumpeterian process of 'creative destruction', in which a competitive business environment allows the entry of new and innovative firms.

2.4.3 Business demography

Analysing the leading indicators of business demography for 2015, which is the last available data, we can see that Greece is characterised by the lowest enterprise birth rate among all countries of the EU (5.1 per cent). The enterprise birth rate is measured as the number of newly born enterprises as a proportion of the total number of active enterprises[1]; it means half of the EU average rate, which was 10.0 per cent. The birth of new enterprises is often seen as one of the critical determinants of job creation and economic growth, since we may assume that new enterprises increase the competitiveness of a country's enterprise population, by obliging them to become more efficient given newly emerging competition. As such, they stimulate innovation and facilitate the adoption of new technologies while helping to increase overall productivity within an economy (Eurostat, 2018).

The average employment size of newly born enterprises in the same year was 1.9 persons. From a theoretical point of view, enterprise birth is related to the expectation of making a profit. If the primary objective of newly born enterprises is to make a profit, enterprise births are most likely to occur where profits are consistently high, whereas among loss-making activities enterprise deaths will be relatively more frequent (Eurostat, 2018). The enterprise death rate[2] in Greece in 2015 was 6.5 compared to 8 per cent in the EU-28 (Eurostat, 2018). It means that in Greece, there were more enterprise deaths than births. Looking at the enterprises' one-year survival rate, it appears that for the business economy about 90 per cent of the enterprises born in 2014 had survived in 2015. In 2015, about 6 per cent of all active enterprises with at least ten employees in Greece business economy were recognised as high-growth enterprises, which means growth in employment by 10 per cent or more. It is about half of EU average. This measure is essential since high growth enterprises rate shows the contribution to the economic growth and the creation of jobs.

2.4.4 Analysis by industry sector

When considering the problem in sectors of activity, we can conclude that the most significant downturn was observed in the construction sector: two-thirds of the enterprises were affected by postponed orders or reservations. The decrease in the number of employees during the years 2008–2016 was 44 per cent and in the value-added creation of 28 per cent. The number of SMEs in this sector decreased by 37 per cent. The main reasons were (1) the collapse of the private construction market after 2009 and (2) replacing of SMEs by large enterprises in smaller construction projects.

SMEs were also affected by the crisis in the manufacturing sector. Overall, during the period 2008–2016, the number of SMEs in this sector decreased by 29 per cent, the number of employees shrank by about 32 per cent, and the value added by about 34 per cent. The main reasons were (1) the austerity measures, particularly tax increases; (2) the reduction of wages and pensions; and (3) reduction in the purchasing power of consumers.

The trade sector recorded heavy losses because of the economic crisis, which is confirmed from the closing of almost 24 per cent of the total number of SMEs during 2008–2016. The employment in trade during this period declined by 19 per cent and the value added by 42 per cent.

The hospitality industry, transportation, and logistics sector recorded relatively small losses compared to the overall economy, with a decline in value added of 14 per cent between 2008 and 2016.

About 20 per cent of the total number of SMEs in 2008 belongs to the high-tech manufacturing and knowledge-intensive services.[3] The vast majority of them operated in knowledge-intensive services (99.5 per cent). During the crisis, the total number of these enterprises decreased by 13 per cent. In 2016, there were 307 SMEs in high-tech manufacturing, and 122,232 operate in knowledge-intensive services compared with 628 and 139,727, respectively, in 2008. This means that the number of companies in the first category has fallen by more than half. They have employed about 15 per cent of total manufacturing and services persons. The share of value added is relatively low (25 per cent) compared to the 33 per cent for the EU in 2016.

2.5 Constraints faced by small and medium enterprises in Greece

Having identified the contributions made by SMEs to employment and value-added creation, we now turn to examining the constraints faced by SMEs in Greece.

The development of SMEs depends on many factors, the impact of which may be constructive (development stimulators) or destructive (development barriers). Here, we deal with the analysis of the barriers to development. Barriers (constraints) contribute to limiting the freedom of managers, hamper development processes, and in some cases lead to crises and collapse of the company. However, some of these barriers may stimulate innovative activities and affect the undertaking of corrective and development actions. In this positive sense, they can be a stimulator of more extensive development efforts taken by the enterprises.

There are many researches concerning the constraints of the functioning of SMEs. It is essential to understand what the key constraints are to analyse the main problems and, in consequence, to decide whether and how SME policies can contribute to eliminating them. These constraints can be divided into internal and external. SMEs are specific participants in the market – they have limited opportunities to influence the external environment. However, any changes taking place in it play a unique role in their functioning. Internal constraints include factors related to the organisational structure, strategy, production capacity, financial, material and human resources, knowledge and technologies, skills and competencies of employees, attitudes and entrepreneurial skills, and more. However, external barriers contain factors regarding the business environment that have an impact between others on the process of setting up and functioning of enterprises on the market. The degree of impact of individual factors depends mostly on the country in which the business is carried out.

Among the external constraints on the development and functioning of SMEs, the following subgroups can be distinguished: legal barriers, technological barriers, socio-cultural barriers, and financial barriers. It should be said that they can be of a general nature or refer to a specific group, for example, industry. The internal barriers to development include the status and quality of tangible and intangible company's resources. Examples of tangible resources are fixed assets and current assets. Investments realised by the company and an effective economy in the area of current assets, with particular emphasis on inventory management, are two main factors which allow maintaining of a company's competitiveness on the market. Intangible assets include the state of human capital, organisation and culture of enterprises, and knowledge and skills of entrepreneurs. Each factor merits thorough consideration and analysis. There are relatively many research studies of this subject concerning SMEs. Much has also been done about the state of the sector in the Greek economy. To analyse these barriers, various indicators and methodologies are used. Each of them has its advantages and disadvantages. Due to the repetitive nature of the research and the possibility of observing changes over time, which is extremely important to the topic given in this book, the conclusions from the research commissioned by the OECD and the European Commission will be mentioned briefly.

The analysis is based in the European context with emphasis on the period 2008–2016.

The constraints preventing enterprises of all size classes from growing are relatively well researched. According to data from the OECD (2017), almost all Greek firms (97 per cent) consider the uncertainty about the future to be an obstacle to investment (Figure 2.7). This share is higher than the

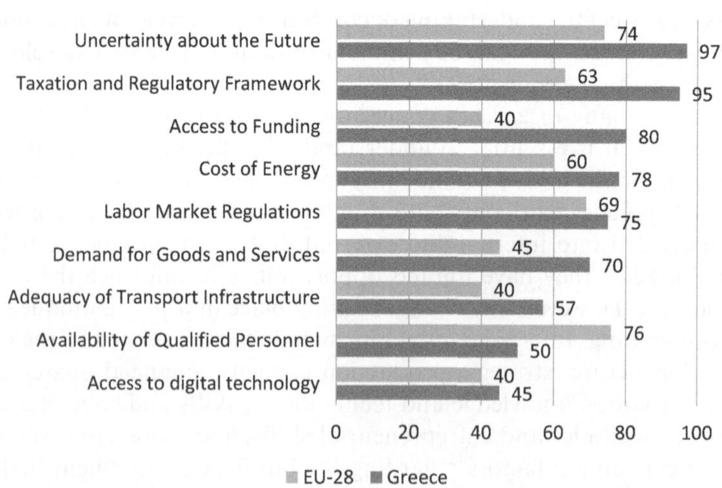

Figure 2.7 Characteristics of the economy that firms face as obstacles to invest (% of enterprises).

Source: OECD (2017).

EU average. Taxation and regulatory framework are also more of a concern for firms in Greece (95 per cent) in comparison with the EU average (63 per cent). Access to funding is perceived as obstacles in Greece in double percentage of firms than across the EU in general. Energy costs, labour market regulations, demand for goods and services, and transport infrastructure are also more likely to be seen to be an obstacle than in the EU.

The three previously mentioned main factors constituting barriers to investment are typical for SMEs as well as for large ones (EIB, 2017).

According to the 2017 SBA Fact Sheet for Greece (EC, 2018), Greece's SME sector performance during 2008–2016 is largely below the EU average. Using compound growth rates for main indicators, the performance in access to finance[4] is the lowest in the EU and the most problematic area for SMEs in Greece, affecting other areas. The second weakest area is SMEs' internationalisation followed by the environment. The single market and 'responsive administration' have been progressing the most since 2008, despite still being below the EU average. In skills and innovation, it scores close to the EU average (Figure 2.8).

As seen in Section 2.3, SMEs constitute the engine of economic growth, most of the new jobs are created in them, and SMEs are flexible and may be easier to adapt to the customers' expectations and the changing business environment. As seen in Section 2.4, Greek SMEs represent a significant share of the economy, accounting for a larger share of total employment and value added than the EU average. The global financial crisis has had profound effects on all sectors and across all economies. With limited capital and resources, SMEs have been particularly impacted by the crisis facing additional obstacles for financing, working capital, and demand. In recent years, the Greek SMEs have borne the brunt of the economic crisis. That is why any barriers that limit their future development or threaten their existence should be systematically analysed and eliminated. In this research, we focus on the barriers of external financing sources. In the next chapter, we explain why bank lending is so crucial for Greek small and medium-sized firms.

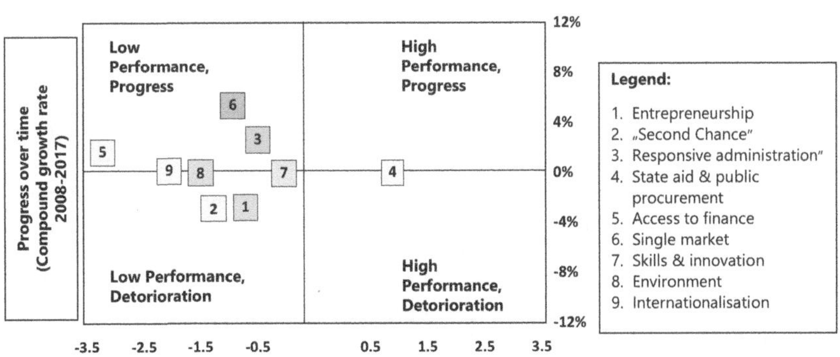

Figure 2.8 SBA performance of Greece, 2008–2017.

Notes

1 An enterprise birth amounts to the creation of a combination of production factors, with the restriction that no other enterprises are involved in the event. Births do not include entries into the business population due to mergers, break-ups, split-offs, or restructuring of a set of enterprises nor do the statistics include entries into a subpopulation that only result from a change of activity. The birth rate is the number of births relative to the stock of active enterprises (Eurostat, 2018).

2 An enterprise death amounts to the dissolution of a combination of production factors, with the restriction that no other enterprises are involved in the event. An enterprise is only included in the count of deaths if it is not reactivated within two years. Equally, a reactivation within two years is not counted as a birth (Eurostat, 2018).

3 The definition of high-tech industries based on the European Commission's SME Performance Review definition (NACE Rev. 2). A statistical classification of economic activities: manufacturing of basic pharmaceutical products and pharmaceutical preparations and manufacturing of computer, electronic, and optical products. Knowledge-intensive services: water transport, air transport, legal and accounting activities, management consultancy activities, activities of head offices; management consultancy activities, architectural and engineering activities; technical testing and analysis, advertising and market research, other professional, scientific and technical activities, employment activities, security and investigation activities, motion picture, video and television programme production, sound recording and music, programming and broadcasting activities, telecommunications, computer programming, consultancy and related activities, information service activities, scientific research and development, publishing activities, and veterinary activities.

4 According to the SBA, the rationale (from COM [2008] 394 final) principles 'access to finance' is 'to facilitate SMEs' access to finance and develop a legal and business environment supportive to timely payments in commercial transactions'.

References

Abor, J., Quartey, A., 2010, Issues in SME development in Ghana and South Africa, *International Research Journal of Finance and Economics*, Vol. 39, pp. 218–228.

Acs, Z.J. (ed.), 1996, *Small Firms and Economic Growth*, Vols. I and II, Edward Elgar Publishers Limited: Cheltenham.

Acs, Z.J., Audretsch, D.B., 1987, Innovation in large and small firms: An empirical analysis, *American Economic Review*, Vol. 78, No. 4, pp. 678–690.

Acs, Z.J., Audretsch, D.B., 1991, *Innovation and Small Firms*, MIT Press: Cambridge.

Acs, Z., Carlsson, B., Karlsson, C., 1999, *Entrepreneurship, Small and Medium-Sized Enterprises, and the Macroeconomy*, Cambridge University Press: Cambridge.

Ang, J.S., 1992, On the theory of finance for privately held firms, *Journal of Small Business Finance*, Vol. 1, No. 3, pp. 185–203.

Audretsch, D.B., 2004, Sustaining innovation and growth: Public policy support for entrepreneurship, *Industry, and Innovation*, Vol. 11, No. 3, pp. 117–126.

Barney, J., 1991, Firms resources and sustained competitive advantage, *Journal of Management*, Vol. 17, No. 1, retrieved on 12/8/2018 from http://business.illinois.edu/josephm/BA545_Fall%202011/S10/Barney%20%281991%29.pdf

Baum, J.A.C., Calabrese, T., Silverman, B.S., 2000, Don't go it alone: Alliance network composition and startups' performance in Canadian biotechnology, *Strategic Management Journal*, Vol. 21, pp. 267–294.

Berisha, G., Pula, J.S., 2015, Defining small and medium enterprises: A critical review, *Academic Journal of Business, Administration, Law and Social Sciences*, Vol. 1, No. 1, pp. 17–28. IIPCCL Publishing, Tirana-Albania.

Bolton, J.E., 1971, *Report of the Committee of Inquiry on Small Firms*, HMSO: London.

Chesbrough, H., 2006, *Open Business Models: How to Thrive in the New Innovation Landscape*, Harvard Business School Press: Boston, MA.

Chittenden, F., Hall, G., Hutchinson, P., 1996, Small firm growth, access to capital markets and financial structure: Review of issues and an empirical investigation, *Small Business Economics*, Vol. 8, pp. 59–67.

Chung, K.H., 1993, Asset characteristics and corporate debt policy: An empirical investigation, *Journal of Business Finance and Accounting*, Vol. 20, No, 4, pp. 83–98.

Committee for Economic Development, 1947, *Meeting the Special Problems of Small Business*, New York.

Cosh, A.D., Hughes, A., 1993, *Size Financial Structure and Profitability: U.K. Companies in the 1980s*, Working Paper, Small Business Research Center, University of Cambridge.

Department of Trade and Industry, 2000a, *Small and Medium Enterprise (SME) Statistics – Definitions*, November 2000 Update, retrieved on 23/8/2018 from www.dti.gov.uk/SME4/smehome.htm

Department of Trade and Industry, 2000b, *Small and Medium Enterprises (SME) Statistics for the UK, 1999*, Department of Trade and Industry Statistical News Release P/2000/561, 7 August 2000.

DIW Econ, 2018, *SME Performance Review 2017*, retrieved on 22/8/2018 from https://diw-econ.de/en/publications/studies/annual-report-on-european-smes-2017-2018/

Dobbs, M., Hamilton, R.T., 2007, Small business growth: Recent evidence and new directions, *International Journal of Entrepreneurial Behaviour & Research*, Vol. 13, No. 5, pp. 296–322.

Dunlop, W., 1992, Small vs. large firms in Australian manufacturing, *Small Business Economics*, Vol. 4, No. 1, pp. 45–58.

EC, 2007, *Eurostat – OECD Manual on Business Demography Statistics*, Office for Official Publications of the European Communities: Luxembourg.

EC, 2016, Statistics on small and medium-sized enterprises, retrieved on 23/8/2018 from https://ec.europa.eu/eurostat/statistics-explained/index.php/Statistics_on_small_and_medium-sized_enterprises#Country_by_country_analysis

EC, 2018, 2017 SBA Fact Sheet, Greece.

EIB, 2017, *EIB Group Survey on Investment and Investment Finance Country Overview: Greece*, European Investment Bank, Ipsos Public Affairs.

European Commission, 1996, *Commission Recommendation of 3 April 1996 Concerning the Definition of Small and Medium-sized Enterprises*, Official Journal of the European Communities, L 107/4, retrieved on 24/8/2018 from http://ec.europa.eu/enterprise/

European Commission, 2003, *Commission Recommendation of 6 May 2003 Concerning the Definition of Micro, Small and Medium-Sized Enterprises*, Official Journal of the European Union.

European Commission, 2005, *The New SME Definition: User Guide and Model Declaration Section*, Office for Official Publications of the European Communities: Brussels.

European Commission, 2014, Commission Regulation (EU) No. 651/2014 of 17 June 2014 declaring certain categories of aid compatible with the internal market in application of Articles 107 and 108 of the Treaty Text with EEA relevance. Official Journal of the European Communities, retrieved on 24/8/2018 from https://eur-lex.europa.eu/

Eurostat, (2016), *Annual Enterprise Statistics for Special Aggregates of Activities*, retrieved on 24/8/2018 from http://ec.europa.eu/eurostat/product?code=sbs_na_sca_r2&language=en&mode=view

Eurostat, 2017, *Business Demography Statistics*, retrieved on 20/8/2018 from https://ec.europa.eu/eurostat/statistics explained/index.php/Business_demography_statistics

Eurostat, 2018, *Small and Medium Enterprises*, retrieved on 24/8/2018 from https://ec.europa.eu/eurostat/web/structural-business-statistics/structural-business-statistics/sme

Gupta, M.C., 1969, The effects of size, growth and industry on the financial structure of manufacturing companies, *Journal of Finance* 24, No. 3, pp. 517–529.

Hellenic Confederation of Professionals, Craftsmen & Merchants (GSEVEE), 2014, *The Development of SMEs in Greece*, The Policy Document, Athens.

Hyz, A., 2010, Technology market in the European Union, *International Business Research*, July, Vol. 3, No. 3, pp. 32–39.

Hyz, A., Gikas, G., 2006, Human capital as the main factor of evolution and trends of regional development – Case of Greece, *The International Journal of Regional Development*, Vol. 20, pp. 34–42.

Independent Evaluation Group, 2008, *Financing Micro, Small and Medium Enterprises: An Independent Evaluation of IFC's Experience with Financial Intermediaries in Frontier Countries*, World Bank Group, retrieved on 24/8/2018 from http://documents.worldbank.org

International Labour Office, 2015, *Small and Medium-Sized Enterprises and Decent and Productive Employment Creation*, International Labour Conference, 104th Session, Geneva.

Johnson, R., Soenen, L., 2003, Indicators of successful companies, *European Management Journal*, Vol. 21, No. 3, pp. 364–369.

Kritikos, A.S., Handrich, L., Mattes, A., 2018, *The Greek Private Sector Remains Full of Untapped Potential*, DIW Weekly Report 29.

Lee, S., Park, G., Yoon, B., Park, J., 2010, Open innovation in SMEs – An intermediated network model, *Research Policy*, Vol. 39, pp. 290–300.

Mulhern, A., 1995, The SME sector in Europe: A broad perspective, *Journal of Small Business Management*, Vol. 33, No. 3, pp. 1–23.

OECD, 1995, *Technology and Economy*, The Key Relationships, Paris, pp. 107 ft.

OECD, 2005, SME and Entrepreneurship Outlook, Paris.

OECD, 2010, *Ministerial Report on the OECD Innovation Strategy*, retrieved on 10/06/2018 from http://www.oecd.org/sti/45326349.pdf

OECD, 2017, *Economic Survey, Greece*, retrieved on 04/09/2018 from www.oecd.org/eco/surveys/economic-survey-greece.htm

OECD/UNIDO, 2004, *Effective Policies for Small Business, A Guide for the Policy Review Process and Strategic Plans for Micro, Small and Medium Enterprise Development*, Paris.

Rothwell, M., Dodgson, J., 1991, External linkages and innovation in small and medium-sized enterprises, *R&D Management*, Vol. 21, No. 2, pp. 125–133.

SBA Fact Sheet for Greece 2017, retrieved from http://ec.europa.eu/enterprise/policies/sme/facts-figures-analysis/performance-review/files/countries-sheets/2017/greece_en.

SBA Fact Sheets for Greece 2008–2018.

SBA, 2013, U.S. *Small Business Administration: Small Business Size Standards*, retrieved on 22/8/2018 from http://www.sba.gov/content/table-small-business-size-standards

Storey, D.J., 1994, *Understanding the Small Business Sector*, International Thomson Business Press: London.

Tamari, M., 1980, The financial structure of the small firm – An international comparison of corporate accounts in the U.S.A., France, U.K., Israel and Japan, *American Journal of Small Business*, April–June, pp. 20–34.

The Commission of the European Communities, Commission Recommendation of 6 May 2003 concerning the definition of micro, small and medium-sized enterprises, *Official Journal of the European Union*, 20.05.2003.

UNIDO, 1999, *Private Sector Development Branch, Investment Promotion and Institutional Capacity Building Division*, retrieved on 24/8/2018 from https://www.unido.org/

Vanhaverbeke, W., 2011, *Beyond Open Innovation in Large Enterprises: How Do Small and Medium-Sized Enterprises (SMEs) Open Up to External Innovation Sources?* Social Sciences Research Network, retrieved on 12/8/2018 from http://papers.ssrn.com/sol3/papers.cfm?abstract_id=1925185

3 Why is bank lending so important in Greece?

3.1 Introduction

One of the main determinants for business start-up, its development, and growth is its access to finance. Small and medium-sized enterprises (SMEs) have very different needs concerning financing compared to large companies. Unlike large firms, small businesses lack access to public institutional debt and equity capital markets, and the vicissitudes of small business profits make retained earnings a significantly less stable source of capital. As a result, the survival and development of these firms are conditioned by providing easy access to financing sources, especially to bank loans which are the most important source of external financing. Bigger companies have been rated by the rating agencies and are the preferred investment vehicles of investors seeking higher returns at a time of low interest rates. On the opposite, small enterprises have relatively restricted access to market financing since there is no information on their intrinsic risk (Nahmias, 2015). In the context of current crisis, the access to bank loans for SMEs has deteriorated significantly due to lower availability of bank loans that can hamper the exit from a crisis of these firms and the national economy. Bank credit, mainly through term loans, is one of the primary sources of external financing for small businesses in the Greek economy, which is characterised by a bank-based financial system. Bank credit is also the key to helping small Greek firms maintain cash flow, hire new employees, purchase new inventory or equipment, and grow their business.

In this chapter, a short presentation of bank-based versus market-based financial system is provided. An analysis of data on small business lending collected by Greek banking regulators is presented. We also provide the results of research on the relationship between banks and SMEs trying to show that the problems of banks' financing of SMEs are a timeless problem. Finally, the new evidence on how the financial crisis affected bank lending to SMEs in Greece is analysed.

3.2 Bank-based financial system versus market-based system

Greek financial system may be characterised as bank-based. In the bank-based financial system, banks play a leading role in mobilising savings, allocating capital, overseeing the investment decisions of corporate managers, and providing risk management vehicles (Demirguc-Kurt and Levine, 1999). In other words, in a bank-based system, financing consists mostly of institutions that conduct financial intermediation on their balance sheet. In general, enterprises in the eurozone rely more heavily on bank financing than their counterparts in the US. Comparing the financial structure of US companies with eurozone companies, we see that in the first case bank loans to the corporate sector as a percentage of the gross domestic product (GDP) is 18.7 per cent and 47.9 per cent in the second case. On the contrary, debt securities issued by the corporate sector in US' companies constitute 41 per cent of GDP and only 10.7 per cent in eurozone companies (Brinkmeyer, 2014). Despite the numerous changes in the Greek financial system, it remains a bank-based system. The Greek banks contribute to the GDP more than 85 per cent of the sector's added value and absorb about 70 per cent of the employees in the financial sector. They provided 93 per cent of the loans to non-financial firms (Argitis and Michopoulou, 2012).

After many years of academic dispute about the pros and cons of a bank-based system and a market-based system, there is no clarity about the advantage of either of them. In the literature, there are more and more views that the competition between the bank- and market-based financial systems is starting to lose terrain due to the process of globalisation. As Levine (2002) stated in his cross-country research, although overall financial development is robustly linked with economic growth, there is no support for either the bank-based or the market-based view. Kashyap and Stein (1994) show that the evidence from the US, as well as other countries, suggests that there is a strong secular trend away from intermediated finance and towards securities markets. However, according to the same authors, in spite of such trends, the data show that intermediaries – and banks in particular – continue to play a dominant role in financing US corporations, particularly medium-sized and smaller ones. They concluded that it seems reasonable to believe that shocks to the supply of intermediated loans might have important aggregate implications, even in today's environment. Corbett and Jenkinson (1997) found that compared with Germany, whose financial system is dominated by banks, bank financing appears to be more important in the UK and almost equally important in the US, even though these countries are considered to have capital market dominated financial systems. Also, Mayer (1990) and Hackethal and Schmidt (1999) support these findings and show that bank credit is still by far the most important source of firms' funding.

It is characteristic that similar views prevail in literature until the last economic crisis in 2008 (Demirguc-Kunt and Levine, 1999; Beck and Levine, 2002, Levine, 2002). As Pagano et al. (2015) stated before the last crisis, banks overextend and misallocate credit in financial upturns and ration credit in financial downturns more than markets. Bats and Houben (2017), exploring the relationship between financial structure and systemic risk, concluded that bank-based financing generates systemic risk while market-based debt and especially market-based stock financing reduce systemic risk. Their findings indicate that countries can increase their resilience to systemic risk by reducing the share of bank-based financing and increasing the share of market-based financing. According to the same authors, the real economic benefits of bank-based financial structures depend on the stability of the financial system, which can be upset by systemic risk with serious negative consequences for the real economy. It was easy to observe, during the recent financial crisis, a drastic drop of the credit flows towards the real economy and the reduced ability and willingness of banks to provide financing.

On the other side, market financing is reserved for the biggest companies because it comes at a cost for the issuer and investors are often more reticent to shoulder risks that are hard to quantify. SMEs cannot adapt to market financing. It is so due to the problem of adverse selection and small amounts of loans, which caused increasing operating and auditing costs. Because banks play a crucial role for SMEs' external financing, bank credit restrictions affect SMEs more severely than large firms. On the other side, the differing financial characteristics of SMEs compared with larger ones and the importance of SMEs within the overall economy show the need to develop a comprehensive range of financial policies and instruments to support SMEs with the most appropriate sources and types of financing at each stage of their life.

3.3 Developments in bank lending in the Greek corporate sector before and during the crisis

Bank lending makes up a preponderant share of the corporate debt of non-financial companies (NFCs; bank lending and debt instruments) for all eurozone member countries. Although there are disparities within the eurozone, as we can see on Figure 3.1, loans from micro finance institutions (MFIs) represent a crucial source of debt funding for eurozone NFCs, especially for SMEs (ECB, 2018, p. 16). In EU-28 countries, the share of bank lending in total debt is 42.3 per cent and in Greece above 70 per cent. Bank loans as a share of the total debt are by far the lowest in countries like Belgium, Luxembourg, Finland, and Denmark. It shows the extreme dependence of Greek NFCs on banking financing sources. It should be stressed that the figure for Greece is the highest among all countries of eurozone and that Greek NFC is mainly financed via the banking channel.

Total outstanding business loans rose without interruption during the period before the financial crisis (Figure 3.2). As a result, the indebtedness of NFCs increased rapidly. From 2006 to 2008, the total outstanding business loans amount raised to over 65 per cent. Loans outstanding were essentially unchanged between 2008 and mid-2009. Since the second half of 2009, they have gradually declined from the high levels accumulated previously. In 2012, it fell by over 20 per cent compared to the beginning of the period. In 2016, it was at the level of 2006. This occurred in an environment that

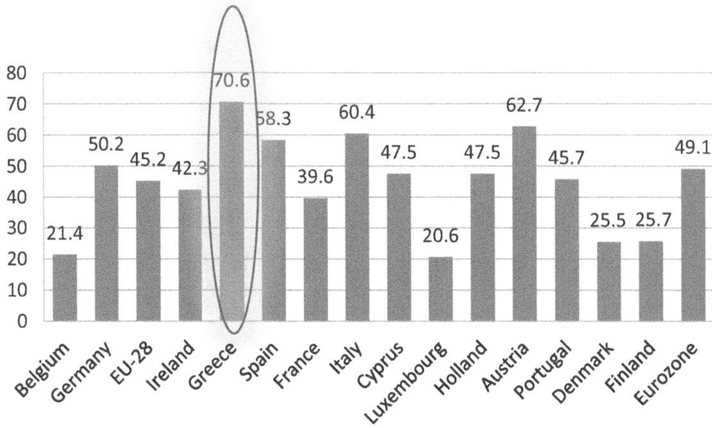

Figure 3.1 Bank lending to non-financial corporations (in total debt, %).
Source: Own calculations based on ECB (2018).

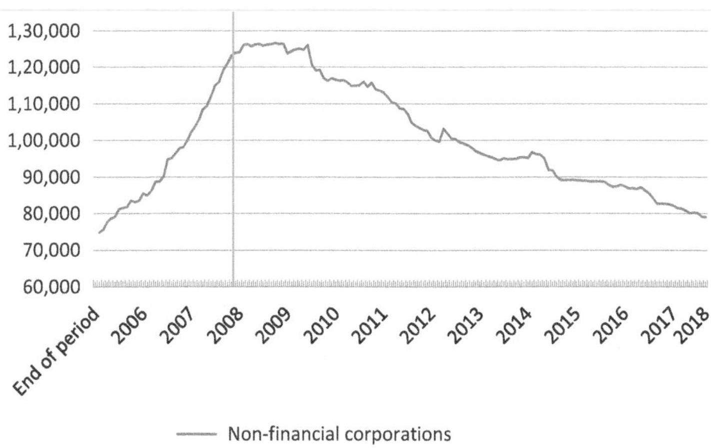

Figure 3.2 Credit to Greek domestic non-MFI residents by domestic MFIs, excluding the Bank of Greece (outstanding amounts at the end of period in EUR millions).
Source: Bank of Greece (2018).

changed with the outbreak of the financial crisis and is characterised by substantially increased credit risk and risk aversion as well as stronger debt sustainability concerns in general (ECB, 2012).

As shown in Figure 3.3, the total outstanding small business lending declined by 14 per cent from 2010 to 2012.[1] They remained low until the end

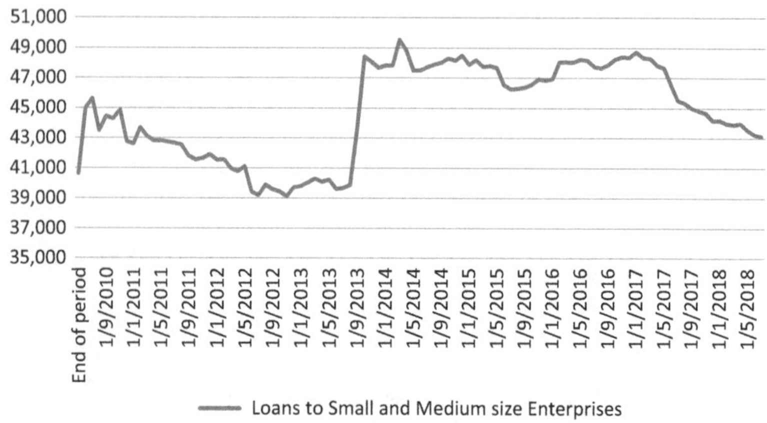

Figure 3.3 Credit to Greek domestic SMEs by domestic MFIs, excluding the Bank of Greece (outstanding amounts at the end of period in EUR millions).
Source: Bank of Greece (2018).

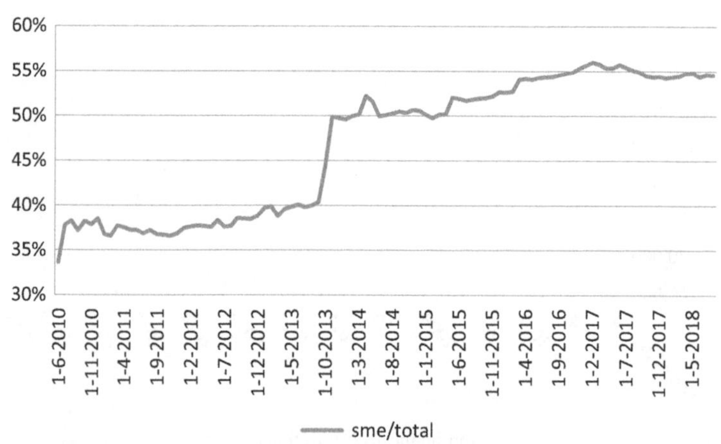

Figure 3.4 The share of outstanding loans to SMEs to total outstanding business lending.
Source: Own calculation based on: Bank of Greece (2018).

of 2013, and then significantly increased in early 2014. Another fall was recorded in 2017. About 40 per cent of total outstanding small business lending referred to short-term loans. The share of outstanding loans for small and medium-sized companies to total outstanding business lending has systematically increased during the period under consideration (Figure 3.4). From 38 per cent in 2010, it rose to 52 per cent in 2014. It achieved the highest share in 2017 (56 per cent) and decreased by 1 per cent point in the last analysed year.

Figure 3.5 illustrates the amount in a million euros of total new business lending and new lending to SMEs in Greece from 2008 to 2016. The flow of new bank loans has dropped sharply from approximately € 36.5 billion in 2008 to € 5.8 billion in 2016. It means a decrease of 84.2 per cent. At the same time, new lending to SMEs decreased from € 12.5 billion in 2008 to under € 1.1 billion in 2016 (decrease of 81.5 per cent). The recession following 2009/2010 is evident, with total new business lending declining from € 36,544 million in 2008 to € 5,771 million in 2016. The share of new lending to SMEs in total new lending dropped from the highest 36 per cent in 2008 to 18.4 per cent in 2016 (Figure 3.6). This evolution described as credit

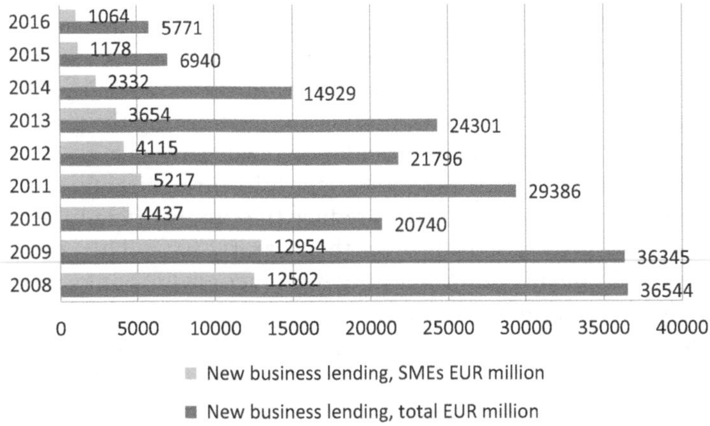

Figure 3.5 New business lending, total and SME, EUR million.
Source: Own calculation based on Bank of Greece (2018).

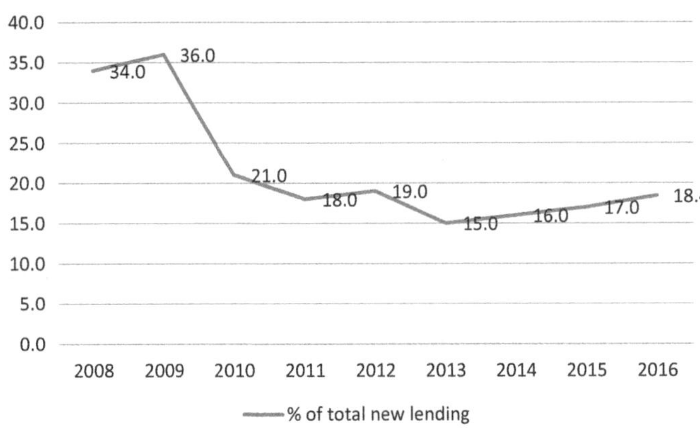

Figure 3.6 Share of SMEs new lending in total new lending.
Source: Own calculation based on Bank of Greece (2018).

crunch means a situation in which the supply of credit is restricted below the range usually identified with prevailing market interest rates and the profitability of investment projects (Bernanke and Gertler, 1995).

It should be noted that the lowest share was in 2013 (15 per cent). The decline in new lending was caused by the combined effect of drop-in credit demand, on one side, and supply-side factors affecting credit to the corporate sector, on the other. As regards the demand side, lower levels of economic activity, high uncertainty, low confidence, the need to reduce the high debt levels, and weaker capital formation have contributed to firms' reduced need for external financing. On the supply side, the tighter credit standards applied by banks have curtailed the growth of bank loans to the non-financial corporate sector (ECB, 2012). As a result of difficult macroeconomic conditions, increasing uncertainty, and need for the rebalancing of lending portfolio, even banks with enough capital for granting loans preferred to avoid risk increasing. Although banks have received significant funding support during the period of crisis, many seek to strengthen their balance sheets to regain access to market funding. The low growth environment, in turn, directly impacts on banks' balance sheet size, as banks reduce the supply of credit, especially when it carries high risk, to protect their capital base. This, in turn, led to a decrease in businesses generating high income for banks, thus worsening their profitability prospects.

When we examine year to year changes in total new lending, we observe significant fluctuation. In 2010, the total volume of new loan contracts

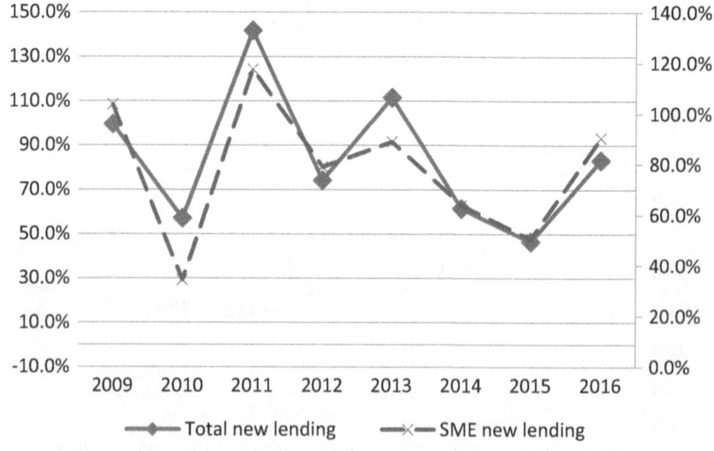

Figure 3.7 Year to year changes in new lending, total and SME.

Source: Own calculation based on Bank of Greece (2018).

Note: This figure shows year to year changes in total new lending shown as bold black line on the left hand and SMEs new lending shown as dotted line on the right hand.

concluded in the past 12 months was lower than that of last year by almost 53 per cent. This index for new lending for SMEs for the same period was 66 per cent (Figure 3.7). Changes which occurred during the next few years have not allowed achieving the before crisis level.

3.4 Credit conditions in the corporate sub-segments

Financial markets in the eurozone progressed steadily towards integration in the years following the introduction of the single currency. This was reflected among others in a convergence of interest rates for private sector loans. However, with the start of the crisis, the banking sector and financial markets gradually fragmented along national borders (European Central Bank [ECB], 2013). The level of fragmentation remains high for the lending to non-financial corporations, as reflected in the widening of interest rate differentials. Interest rates for one-year loans up to € 1 million was 5 per cent in Greece, while SMEs in France, Belgium, and Luxembourg reporting rates were around 2 per cent in 2015 (Figure 3.8).

In Greece, net lending conditions have been deteriorating since the second half of 2008, with the lessening of the negative trend between 2009 and the first half of 2012. After that, interest rates started to fall. The highest interest rates spread was in 2010 (1.26 per cent points; Figure 3.9). The spread may be used as a measure of the borrowing terms for small businesses and show to which extent the borrowing terms are more restrictive than those for larger firms during the same period. It is worth noting that although interest rates decreased, the lending amounts also decreased (Figure 3.10). It indicates that lower interest rates do not reduce the financial constraints of the SMEs.

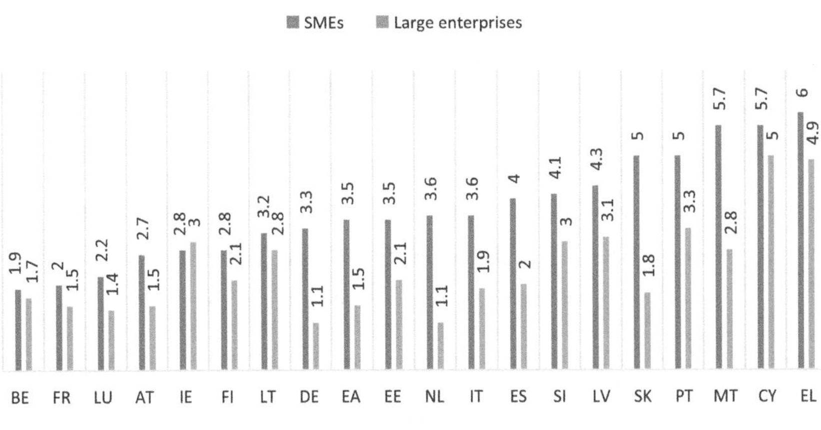

Figure 3.8 Interest rates for one-year loans, in % (February 2015).
Source: ECB (2017)a.

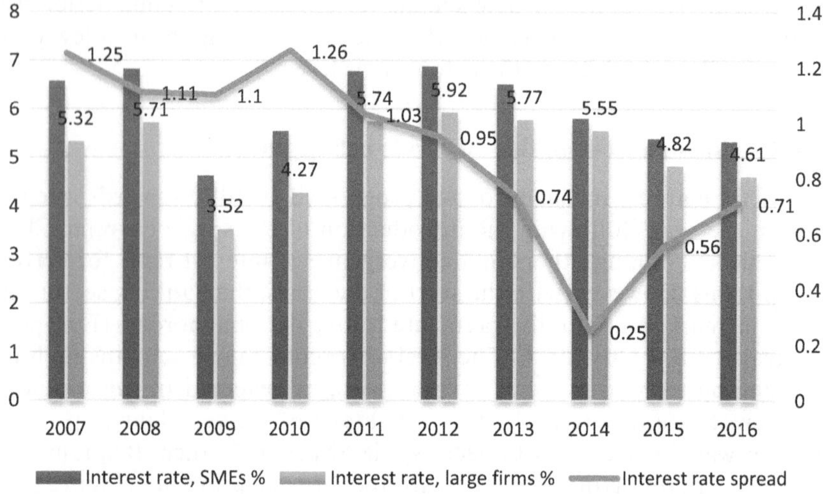

Figure 3.9 Interest rates and interest rate spread, large firms and SMEs.

Source: Bank of Greece (2018).

Note: This figure shows interest rate for SMEs shown as black bar on the left line, interest rate for large firms shown as grey bar on the left hand, and interest spread shown as grey line on the right hand.

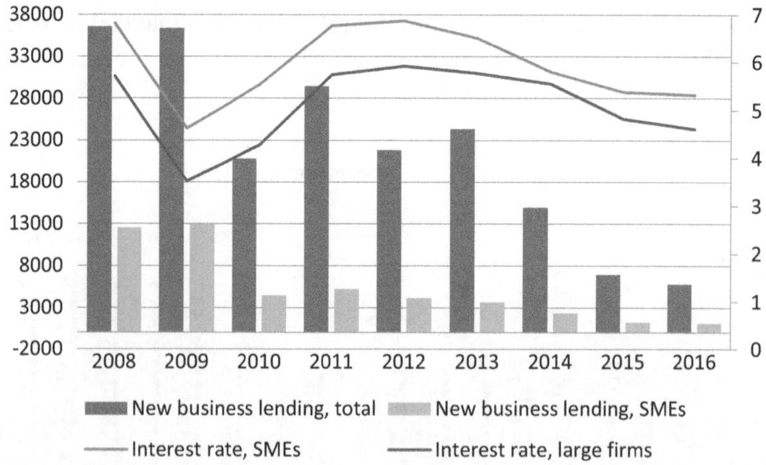

Figure 3.10 Relationships between new lending for large firms and SMEs and interest rates.

Source: Own calculation based on Bank of Greece (2018).

Note: This figure shows relationships between new lending for large firms shown as black bar on the left hand, new business lending for SMEs shown as grey bar on the left hand, interest rate for large firms shown as black line on the right hand, and interest rate for SMEs shown as grey line on the right hand.

During the period under consideration, government loan guarantees to SMEs loans decreased from € 19.9 billion to € 12.8 billion, which means a decrease of almost 45 per cent.

BOX 3.1 BANK LENDING SURVEY – THE OVERVIEW (ECB, 2017A)

The main object of the eurozone bank lending survey (BLS), which was launched by the eurosystem in 2003, is to enhance its knowledge of bank lending conditions. It provides information on the lending policies of eurozone banks and complements existing statistics on loans and bank lending rates with information on loan supply and demand for enterprises and households. The survey is conducted four times a year and is addressed to senior loan officers of a representative sample of eurozone banks, which comprises around 150 banks from all eurozone countries. The BLS contains 18 backward-looking questions and 4 forward-looking questions (expected development). The survey distinguishes between three loan categories: loans or credit lines to enterprises, loans to households for house purchase, and consumer credit and another lending to households. The survey includes questions on credit standards for approving loans, credit terms and conditions on new loans, loan demand, the factors affecting loan supply and demand conditions, and the share of loan rejections.

Credit standards are the internal guidelines or loan approval criteria of a bank. They are applied before negotiations on the terms and conditions of a loan begin, and the loan application is approved or rejected. Credit terms and conditions refer to the terms and conditions of the loan as laid down in the loan contract between the bank (the lender) and the borrower. They include, for instance, the loan margin, the collateral required, and the maturity of the loan. The BLS also includes questions asking banks to assess how specific factors affect the credit standards they apply when approving loans to enterprises and households and how these factors affect the terms and conditions of new loans. Concerning loan demand and the various factors that may affect it, the BLS focuses on the need of enterprises and households for bank loan financing, irrespective of whether a loan is granted. In addition to the questions on loan demand, banks are asked to assess the impact of various factors related to the financing needs of enterprises and households and the use of alternative sources of financing. Survey participants indicate changes on a five-point scale: (1) tightened/decreased considerably, (2) tightened/decreased somewhat, (3) basically unchanged, (4) eased/increased somewhat, or (5) eased/increased considerably. The results of the individual banks participating in the BLS sample are aggregated to national results and to eurozone BLS results.

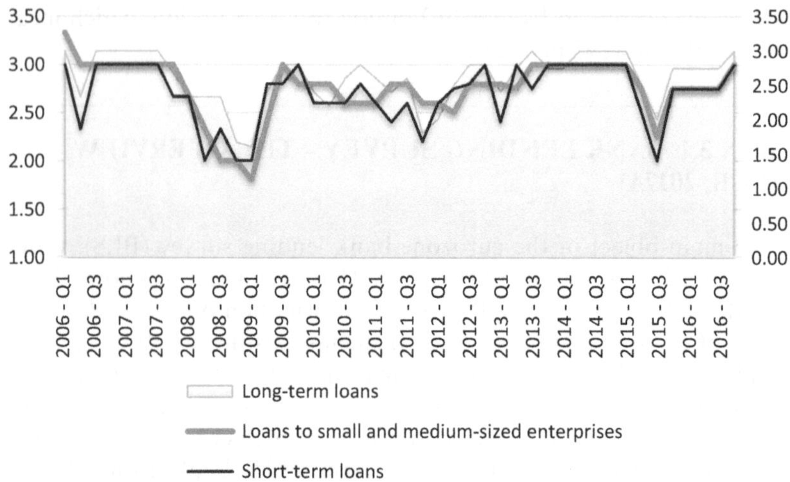

Figure 3.11 Changes in bank's credit standards for approving loans or credit lines to enterprises.

Source: Own calculation based on bank lending survey (BLS), ECB (2018).

Note: This figure shows changes in bank's credit standards for approving loans or credit lines to SMEs shown as the red line on the left hand, short-term loans which is shown as the black line on the left hand, and long-term loans shown as grey area on the right hand.

Credit standards for approving loans or credit lines to Greek SMEs during the period under investigation were decreasing till the first quarter of 2009, when they reached the lowest level (Figure 3.11). During 2009, they increased significantly and remained almost unchanged, with some fluctuations, until the first quarter of 2015. They were tightened more strongly on loans to SMEs than on loans to large firms. When we talk about credit standards, we mean the internal guidelines or loan approval criteria of a bank established prior to the actual loan negotiation on the terms and conditions and the actual loan approval/rejection decision.

Among the factors driving the tightened credit standards in a bank, costs related to the bank's capital position and the perception of risk[2] (general economic situation and outlook and risk related to the collateral demanded) are the most critical factors. It should be noted that the cost related to the bank's capital position can become a balance sheet constraint that may inhibit the expansion of its lending. The bank's loan supply, for a given level of capital, could be affected by its liquidity position and its access to money and debt markets. Similarly, risks related to non-performing loans may be reflected in its cost of funds and balance sheet constraints. During the period under investigation, pressure from competition (other banks, nonbanks, and market financing) decreased significantly in the third quarter of 2011 and remained unchanged during the rest of the period.

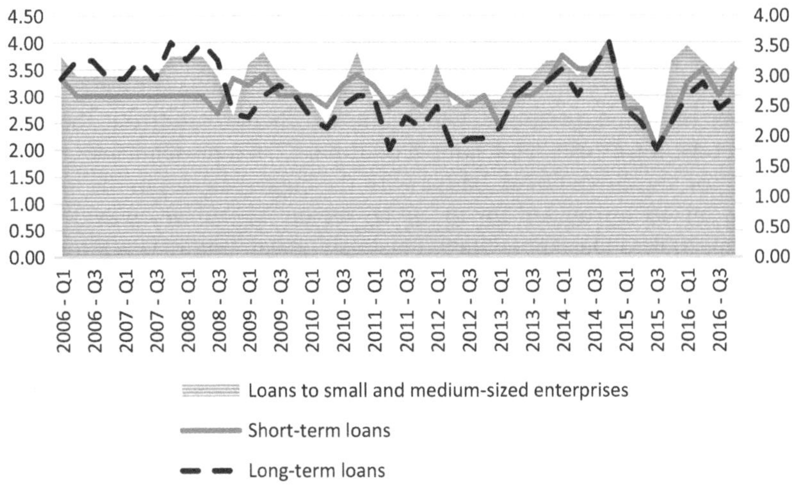

Figure 3.12 Changes in demand for loans or credit lines to enterprises, apart from normal seasonal fluctuations.

Source: Own calculation based on bank lending survey (BLS), ECB (2018).

Note: This figure shows changes in demand for loans or credit lines to enterprises in three dimensions. Loans to SMEs shown as grey area on the right hand, short-term loans shown as the dotted black line on the left hand, and long-term loans shown as the grey line on the left hand.

Net demand for loans to enterprises or credit lines to enterprises decreased significantly in 2008 and remained weak till the end of 2015 (Figure 3.12). Loan demand increased for both short- and long-term loans during 2016. The weak demand was mainly due to the general level of interest rates and the small contribution of fixed investment. The use of alternative finance has a little effect on net loan demand from small and medium-sized businesses.

3.5 The relationship between Greek SMEs and banks – some remarks from the before crisis period

In this part, the results of the survey developed during the non-crisis period in Greece are presented. The aim is to analyse the relationship between Greek SMEs and banks and to describe the main factors restricting the access of Greek SMEs to banking services. Specific characteristics of SMEs – their size and a big diversity of economic units – with a big growth potential cause that they should constitute for banks a desirable group of clients. Meanwhile, the situation looks different. Cooperation between banks and Greek SMEs, during the period considered, was highly unsatisfactory. The gaps in the financing of SMEs were observed, both in the start-up phase and in later growth. Our research was carried out to identify the causes of such a situation.

3.5.1 Methodology

The analysis is based upon a special questionnaire through which the problem of SME financing was investigated. The questionnaire surveys were arranged in such a way that representatives of banks and SMEs were expected to answer the same questions, which allowed them to confront their opinions directly. It was used as a sample of almost 250 representatives from the SME sector and three Greek banks with the biggest shares in the market of banking services provided for the SME sector. The survey was developed from June 2008 to December 2009. The draft questionnaire was piloted in 10 per cent of the survey and subsequently amended in the light of the findings from the pilot. The survey was designed to be sent by mail. However, because of the specific nature of SMEs' business culture and based on the experience of previous surveys, we decided to conduct the survey by telephone.

3.5.2 Results

Around 42 per cent of the managers surveyed feel that the offer from the banks was not suited to their needs. In other words, a key factor was a small demand of SMEs for services offered by banks. In general, only about 23 per cent of an SME's turn first to banks when they look for information or advice about financing. According to enterprises, the next barriers in access to banking services were high costs of bank loans, collateral required by banks, and complicated and time-consuming procedures connected with obtaining bank loans. According to the survey, almost 7 per cent of SMEs representatives believed that banks request too much information, the administrative side of the loan application was very demanding (59 per cent), the loan granting procedures were too long (47 per cent), and around a third feel that interest rates were too high (32 per cent). These restrictions were faced, first of all, by the smallest firms and business start-ups. Whereas it can hardly be expected that banks should simplify their procedures and lower the level of required collateral considering only the firm size, it can be expected that costs of obtaining bank loans should decrease in the longer perspective. Taking into consideration the fact that SMEs have very limited possibilities of their development relying solely on their own capital, unavailability of loans in the domestic financial market, including investment loans, poses a major barrier reducing development potential of SMEs. It should be noted that many of the SMEs included in the survey did not have a development plan for the coming years (65 per cent). The likelihood that a company had a development plan decreases as the number of years it has existed goes up and increases as turnover and employment increases. The third place was taken by major discrepancies in evaluations given by both sides. According to enterprises, arduous banking procedures were a significant barrier, although the managers in Greece were most likely to feel that compared to a few years ago it was easier to obtain a bank loan (85 per cent).

Meanwhile, banks claim the weaknesses from the financial management viewpoint which include small ability to accumulate financial surpluses not giving a guarantee that the invested capital will be returned; high costs of firms' operation and low profitability; constraints connected with a specific financial management in firms; and low level of managerial skills of owners and management. In the opinion of the banks, SMEs were not prepared properly to use banking services. The next question was addressed solely to enterprises concerning a discriminatory treatment of SMEs by banks during the evaluation of loan applications. The answers should induce banks to draw more serious conclusions: 92.4 per cent of entrepreneurs confirmed that such discrimination did exist, while 76.7 per cent pointed to a harmful character of such discriminatory activities. Banks were asked a question concerning the reliability of data to be found in documents submitted by entrepreneurs. Banks assessed the reliability of data submitted by micro firms at the level of 2.5 points and the reliability of data submitted by SMEs at 3.6 points (on the five-point scale). Entrepreneurs, in turn, stated that it was very difficult or impossible to conceal any information, as banks analysed and verified the credibility of the documents very carefully (in the opinion of 96.6 per cent of all respondents). Another problem raised by firms was the fact that banks are not elastic in the situation when a debtor faces liquidity problems. Half of the interviewed firms assessed that the possibilities of negotiating the repayment of loan rules were very poor. Banks in their questionnaire identified conditions determining possibilities of loan restructuring, which include the debtor's present financial situation and the possibility of debt restructuring and the history of cooperation.

It is also worth to conclude that:

1. Firms in the SME sector display evident unwillingness to seek external sources of capital. The most important role was played by the owners' financial resources and retained earnings. Loans taken by them were usually needed to maintain their liquidity and more seldom for investment projects. It was primarily due to a conviction prevailing among SMEs that procedures of granting loans were very complicated, loan costs were high, and small firms were discriminated.
2. Banks did not generally distinguish in their policy specific aspects of the SME sector and its growing diversity – a major advantage of very small firms and the fact that a significant share of these firms were young firms.
3. The survey indicates that young companies were more likely to open up or increase capital than those that have been operating for many years. Among SMEs that have operated for 30 years or more, one in six affirms this intention in the future compared to about one in three SMEs that have existed for less than 30 years. Companies that have seen an increase in the number of employees in the past year were significantly more likely to consider opening up or increasing their capital (37 per cent)

than were companies where the number of employees has stayed unchanged or decreased (26 per cent and 28 per cent, respectively).

4 SMEs and, particularly, young and very small firms did not have a positive experience from their cooperation with banks, and such experience did not encourage them to intensify their cooperation with banks. Cooperation with banks did not usually constitute an integral element in the development strategy of SMEs. It was based, in most cases, on seeking a bank's assistance in critical situations and not on partnership relations, from which both sides can derive definite advantages.

5 Despite the importance of innovative SMEs, they faced problems when attempting to access financing as they represent a higher risk than traditional SMEs or large firms.

Notes

1 From 2010, lending for small and medium-sized companies is noted in the statistics of Bank of Greece.

2 Perception of risk refers to the bank's perception of actual risk and its reaction to the developments associated to the general economic situation and outlook, the industry or firm-specific situation and outlook, and the borrower's creditworthiness as well as the collateral demanded (demand-side factors). By contrast, risk tolerance refers to the risk tolerance of the bank in its lending policy, which may alter due to changes in the bank's underlying business strategy (supply-side factors). Banks' perception of actual risk and their risk tolerance may either change in line with each other or move in different directions (ECB, 2017a).

References

Argitis, G., Michopoulou, S., 2012, Financialization and the Greek Financial System, *Studies in Financial Systems*, No. 4.

Bank of Greece, 2018, Credit Aggregates, retrieved on 12/10/2018 from https://www.bankofgreece.gr/pages/en/statistics/monetary/financing.aspx

Bats, J., Houben, A., 2017, *Bank-Based versus Market-Based Financing: Implications for Systemic Risk*, De Nederlandsche Bank Working Paper No. 577.

Beck, T., Levine, R., 2002, *Industry Growth and Capital Allocation: Does Having a Market- or Bank- Based System Matter?* Working Paper 8982, National Bureau of Economic Research, June 2002, retrieved on 12/06/2018 from https://www.nber.org/papers/w8982.pdf

Bernanke, B.S., Gertler, M., 1995, Inside the black box: The credit channel of monetary transmission, *Journal of Economic Perspectives*, Vol. 9, No. 4, pp. 27–47.

Brinkmeyer, H., 2014, *Driver of Bank Lending. New Evidence from the Crisis*, Springer Gabler: Wiesbaden.

Corbett, J., Jenkinson, J., 1997, How is investment financed? A study of Germany, Japan, the United Kingdom, and the United States, Blackwell Publishers Ltd and The Victoria University of Manchester, pp. 69–93.

Demirguc-Kurt, A., Levine, R., 1999, *Bank-Based and Market-Based Financial Systems: Cross-Country Comparisons*, Policy Research Working Papers, World Bank Group.

ECB, 2012, Corporate Indebtedness in the Euro Area, Monthly Bulletin, retrieved on 22/08/2018 from https://www.ecb.europa.eu/pub/pdf/other/art2_mb201202en_pp87-103en.pdf?6dbada7117cef9edf587cdb1bef279a8

ECB, 2013, Annual Report 2013, retrieved on 23/08/2019 from https://www.ecb.europa.eu/pub/pdf/annrep/ar2013en.pdf

ECB, 2017a, User guide to the euro area bank lending survey, European Central Bank – Eurosystem, retrieved on 23/07/2018 from https://www. Ecb.europa.eu/stats/pdf/bls_user_guide_201811.en.pdf

ECB, 2017b, Euro area bank interest rate statistics, retrieved on 12/10/2018 from https://www.ecb.europa.eu/press/pdf/mfi/mir1804.pdf

ECB, 2018, Euro area bank lending survey, retrieved on 12/07/2018 from https://www.bankofgreece.gr/Pages/en/Statistics/monetary/Bank LendingSurvey.aspx

Hackethal, A., Schmidt, R.H., 1999, *Financing Patterns: Measurement Concepts and Empirical Results*, University of Frankfurt, 15 March, pp. 1–15.

Kashyap, A.K., Stein, J.C., 1994, Monetary policy and bank lending, *NBER Studies in Business Cycles*, Vol. 29, pp. 221–256.

Levine, R., 2002, Bank-based or market-based financial systems: Which is better? *Journal of Financial Intermediation*, Vol. 11, No. 4, pp. 398–428.

Mayer, C., 1990, Financial systems, corporate finance, and economic development, in Hubbard, R.G., ed., *Asymmetric Information, Corporate Finance, and Investment,* University of Chicago Press: Chicago, IL, pp. 307–332.

Nahmias, L., 2015, *Corporate Financing in the Eurozone: Recent Trends and Prospects*, BNP Paribas, pp. 1–21.

Pagano, M., Langfield, S., Acharya, V., Boot, A., Brunnermeier, M., Buch, C., Hellwig, M., Sapir, A., van der Burg, I., 2015, *Is Europe Overbanked?* The European Systemic Risk Board's Advisory Scientific Committee Report, No. 4.

4 State of Greek banking sector

Supply side

4.1 Introduction

An efficient and competitive banking sector has a significant contribution to economic growth. Banks provide financial services necessary for enterprises and households to undertake their business, intermediate savings to productive investment through the credits supply, and enable risk sharing. The efficient operation of the financial system ensures a steady stream of income and expenditure in the economic circuit. An enhancement in bank performance is strongly associated with a more efficient apportionment of financial resources and a rise in investments in favour of economic growth and prosperity. On the contrary, an inefficient financial system disrupts the distribution of productive resources and causes large fluctuations in the product, employment, and price levels in the economy. The contribution of the efficient functioning of the financial sector to economic growth has been widely established in the empirical literature (King and Levine, 1993; Levine, 1997; Levine and Zervos, 1998).

Traditionally, banks have been considered to be potentially more vulnerable to instability than other industries (Carletti and Hartmann, 2002). The main reasons are: (1) A bank's balance sheet consists of short-term deposits on the liability side and long-term assets that can be difficult to liquidate quickly. (2) Highly leveraged firms have an incentive to engage in risky behaviour. This phenomenon known as agency problems is particularly strong for banks (Kaufman, 1995; Zawalinska, 1999). The instability in the banking system can have more debilitating effects than instability in other industries. Bank failures can have substantial economic costs and, since the banks are connected through a variety of networks, a shock to one bank can lead to shocks to other banks (Northcott, 2004). The banking sector's performance is often perceived as the replica of economic activities of the economy, as a healthy banking system plays as the bedrock of economic, social, and industrial growth of an economy. Policymakers should aim to facilitate a banking system that supports both economic efficiency and stability. The most crucial question is: what is the optimal competitive structure to promote efficiency and stability?

After the mid-1980s and till the 2000s, the Greek financial system has adjusted to the regulatory framework of the European Union (EU). The main characteristic of this period was the liberalisation, the modernisation, and the internationalisation of the banking sector. The effect of changes as well as favourable macroeconomic conditions was an increase in profitability, especially in the 2000s. However, with the start of the crisis, Greek banks experienced significant falls in their profitability. The situation in the Greek banking sector during the years of the crisis was characterised by consolidation process and concentration, worsening of the banks' financial situation, increasing of Non-Performing Loans (NPLs), a decrease in deposits by domestic enterprises and households, and the parallel increase in loan's interest rate.

This chapter presents the evolution of the Greek banking sector during the economic crisis, its structure today and financial situation according to the CAMELS methodology. This chapter is organised into the following sections. The first section sets out the theoretical underpinnings of the banking consolidation process. It also spells out the motives and factors driving mergers and acquisitions (M&As) and the various methods of consolidation. Trends in M&A activity and the progress in banking consolidation in Greece are detailed in the next section. The impact of the consolidation process on competition in the Greek banking sector and efficiency of the merged entities is analysed in section five. The final section briefly sets out the conclusions.

4.2 Banking consolidation process

There are several alternative methods of consolidation. Each of them has its strengths and weaknesses, depending on the situation. The most common methods are M&As. The acquisition refers to acquiring control of one corporation by another and merger is a particular type of acquisition that results in a combination of both the assets and liabilities of acquired and acquiring firms (Hunsaker and Coombs, 1988; Shull and Hanweck, 2001; Romanyuk, 2010). M&As have become the most important strategic element driving business growth and excellence. M&As will continue to be an ever-present characteristic of the modern corporate landscape. The organisation taking place in the M&As aims to benefit from the synergies of merging firms by rationalisation and integration of the people, processes, and technologies. In an era of increasing globalisation and competitiveness, M&As are considered as a strategic driver for market dominance, geographical expansion, competence, leverage in resource, and capability acquisition (Cartwright and Cooper, 1994). M&As in the financial sector, in particular the banking sector, can increase expected profits by reducing expected costs or by increasing expected revenues or a combination of both (King and Levine, 1993). Cost reduction through M&As could arise for several reasons, including economies of scale, economies of scope, infusing efficient management, and reduction and diversification of risk due to geographic or product diversification (Rosenbaum and Joshua, 2009). The success of M&A depends on a number of factors. The main factors are the development of a strategic programme of an acquisition before its implementation, the optimal selection of a partner and accurate analysis, the appropriate evaluation of the expected synergies, the effective realisation of the connection, and the establishment of a reasonable transaction price (Bertoncelj and Kovac, 2007; Pikula, 2008; Chambers and Honeycutt, 2009). It is reported that one of the main reasons for the failure of a merger or acquisition is based on human resources problems (Hyz, 2009). People issues have been the most sensitive but often ignored issues in a merger and acquisition (Cartwright and Cooper, 1994; Anderson, 1999; Wiley, 2004). M&As of foreign companies are much more complicated than M&As made on a domestic market. It is due to the differences in the business environment (political, economic, organisational, and cultural factors; Sudarsanam, 2003; Hyz, 2009).

Market structure and competition in the European financial sector are major economic policy issues. Competition in the financial sector matters for a number of reasons. As in other industries, the degree of competition in the financial sector may influence the efficiency of the production of financial services. Also, as in other industries, it can affect the quality of financial products and the degree of innovation in the sector. Specific to the financial sector is the link between competition and stability. As for other industries, M&As in the banking sector generate a trade-off between gains and adverse effects. The effects of consolidation can be positive as larger banks may be more efficient and profitable than smaller ones and generate economies of scale and scope. Furthermore, the reorganisation of the merged/acquired bank can have a positive impact on its managerial efficiency. If the concentration generates efficiency gains and these are transferred to the customers, they may benefit from lower prices and higher quality services, as the range of products and services provided by larger banks is supposedly wider than what is offered by smaller banks.

On the other hand, the concentration may increase the market power of merged institutions. The process of consolidation can also cause a reduction in the credit supplied to some categories of borrowers, particularly small firms, new firms, and those with a small number of lenders (Strahan and Weston, 1996; Walraven, 1997; Zardkoohi and Kolari, 1997; Strahan and Weston, 1998; Neviana, 2003). Financial consolidation has implications for competition and also for financial stability, monetary policy, and efficiency of financial institutions (Bikker and Bos, 2004; Prasad and Ghosh, 2005; Cartwright and Schoenberg, 2006; DePamphilis, 2008). Due to the diverse nature of financial institutions, different levels of financial development, and different legal frameworks, the causes and impact of financial consolidation vary across the countries. The relationships between competition, banking system performance, and stability have been extensively analysed in the theoretical literature. The impact of consolidation through M&As on competition operates through a number of channels and depends mainly on the market structure, the nature of competition, and the regulatory and supervisory framework. A good deal of debate on competition effects of bank consolidation has been phrased regarding two competing hypotheses. The structure–conduct–performance paradigm argues that concentration will intensify market power and thereby stymie competition and efficiency. In contrast, the efficiency paradigm argues that economies of scale drive bank M&As, so that increased concentration goes hand in hand with efficiency improvements.

The empirical research on the issue of competition, particularly cross-country research, is still in an early stage. Most of these studies find that M&As may have influenced market prices. In the US, a reduction in the interest rate on deposits is detected in markets that have been affected by consolidation (Prager and Hannan, 1998). Financial consolidation led to higher concentration in countries such as the US and Japan, though they continue to have much more competitive banking systems as compared with other countries (Kenneth and Critchfield, 2005). However, in several other countries, the process of consolidation led to a decline in banking concentration, reflecting an increase in competition (Prasad and Ghosh, 2005). Estimates of the impact of mergers on prices for the Swiss retail banking market indicate that concentration may have a negative effect on prices (Egli and Rime, 1999). In the M&As in Italy, loan rates increase when the market share of the acquired bank is large (Sapienza, 2002). The indirect approach using European data generally finds that higher concentration leads to less favourable conditions for bank customers (Hempell, 2002; Gutiérrez de Rozas, 2007). Market power in connection with prices for small business loans and retail deposits is found to exist in both the US and Europe (Berger and Hannan, 1989). For the Latin American banking system, it was found that (i) concentration in banking markets did not necessarily lead to a lower level of competition and higher bank performance, and (ii) bank returns were negatively linked to the degree of competition and, to a lower extent, to foreign bank participation (Yildirim and Philippatos, 2007; Hyz, 2011).

Furthermore, in the context of the Latin American banking system, Yeyati and Micco (2007) suggested that it not be at all clear whether competition and concentration should go in opposite directions. Carletti and Hartmann (2002), who have investigated the trade-off between competition and concentration, have found that there is no evidence that the banking sector concentration relates negatively to the level of competition. In a cross-country study using structural model covering 50 major advanced and emerging market economies, Claessens and Laeven (2003) found that lower activity restrictions in the banking sector and greater foreign bank presence make banking systems more competitive. However, they found no evidence that banking system concentration was negatively associated with competition. Considering the internationalisation of banking sector in Turkey, Abbasoglu et al. (2007) found no evidence of the existence of a relationship between consolidation and competition. However, even for countries where the consolidation process is more advanced, namely Argentina and Mexico, no noticeable impact of consolidations on competition intensity has been found (Gaston-Gelos and Roldos, 2002). Bank consolidation in most emerging economies has not yet been associated with any marked rise in concentration, as most mergers appeared to have involved smaller banks. One reason for this pattern could have been reluctance on the part of the authorities to sanction mergers between the largest banks, which could raise both competition and moral hazard concerns. An important point that the recent literature on concentration-competition suggests is that the number of banks and the degree of concentration are not, in themselves, sufficient indicators of contestability. Other factors play an active role, including regulatory policies that promote competition, a well-developed financial system, the effects of branch networks, and the effect and uptake of technological advancements (Northcott, 2004).

Because concentration measures do not necessarily provide a good indication of market contestability, many recent studies of banking markets have applied techniques such as the Panzar-Rosse H-statistic (Panzar and Rosse, 1987). This is a measure of competition based on the estimated responsiveness of firm's revenue to changes in factor input prices.[1] The Panzar and Rosse (P-R) methodology enables to identify the nature of the market structure, that is, oligopoly, monopoly competition, or perfect competition, by applying the elasticity of total interest revenues function for changes in the banks' input prices (Gaston-Gelos and Roldos, 2002; Bikker, 2004). Despite the limitations, the model's special advantages make it a valuable tool in assessing market conditions. The P-R methodology analyses directly the competitive conduct of banks, based on the comparative static properties of the reduced form of revenue function, without employing any structural measures (Koutsomanoli-Fillipaki and Staikouras, 2004). The Herfindahl-Hirschman Index (HHI) can measure the concentration of the banking sector. The HHI is defined as the sum of the squares of the market shares of the 50 largest firms (or summed over all the firms if there are fewer than 50) within the industry, where the market shares are expressed as percentages (Hirschman, 1964). The result is proportional to the average market share, weighted by market share. Increases in the Herfindahl Index generally indicate a decrease in competition. H* index below 0.01 (or 100) indicates a highly competitive index, H* index below 0.1 (or 1,000) indicates an unconcentrated index, H* index between 0.1 to 0.18 (or 1,000–1,800) indicates moderate concentration, and H* index above 0.18 (above 1,800) indicates high concentration.

4.3 Macroeconomic situation in Greece – the background

The global and economic crisis which began in 2008 with the depth and severity of economic slowdown has caught governments, companies, investors, and consumers by surprise. The current crisis is the biggest one the world economy has experienced since the Second World War. Due to the increased integration of goods, services, and financial markets, as we described in Chapter 1, the crisis has spread from housing and credit sectors in the US to other markets and countries around the world. There are few, if any, economies that have been left untouched by the crisis. The international financial system has reached the brink of collapse, which has been avoided thanks to interventions by governments and central banks.

In the period 2002–2007, there was the highest average global growth rate over the last 40 years. At the same time, the global economy and the international capital markets were overwhelmingly optimistic about the prospects of the economies.

The collapse of Lehman Brothers has denied the legend that there are banking institutions that are 'too big to fail', causing panic in the international financial market. It became clear that the funds held by the banks are inadequate concerning the assumed risk. As a result, uncertainty in the financial markets increased and liquidity declined. Banks have restricted lending to households and businesses, leading to a reduction in investment and employment. The deterioration of the macroeconomic situation could not be without impact on the fiscal policies of the countries of the EU. The effect was twofold.

On the one hand, the state was forced to recapitalise the banks threatened with bankruptcy. The improvement in the financial sector was aimed at restoring the borrowing of the real economy. The scale of the aid granted to the banks was unprecedented, since in 2008–2010 it reached 2.35 per cent of the GDP of 2010 of all the countries of the EU.

On the other hand, the crisis, through the operation of automatic stabilisers of the economy, has led to a significant deterioration in the budgetary situation of the Member States of the EU. In many countries, the general government deficit has reached very high levels, significantly higher than those required by the Stability and Growth Pact. As a result, the European states, some of which were already deficient, have to bear extra debts and have the burden of recession on the citizens. In April 23, 2010, when Greece was unable to refinance its debt in the financial market, it requested assistance from other members of the eurozone and the International Monetary Fund. Shortly after, similar problems arose in Ireland and Portugal, with simultaneous increases in borrowing costs in Italy and Spain. In this way, the financial crisis has put Europe in a debt crisis, threatening the process of monetary consolidation. In 2009, Greece was hit by the economic crisis, and during the next few years, the Greek economy was characterised by a decrease of GDP (Figure 4.1).

The characteristic feature of the Greek labour market during the last few years was relatively low employment. Analysing the period under investigation, we can observe that the total employment in the Greek economy in 2016 decreased by about 1 million people in comparison with 2008, reaching 3.6 million. It is worth noting that in 2013, due to the decline in employment, the ratio of employees to total economically active population was only 52.2 per cent. It means a decrease by almost 11 points compared to 2008, which then ranged around 63 per cent (Table 4.1). It was mostly the effects of the

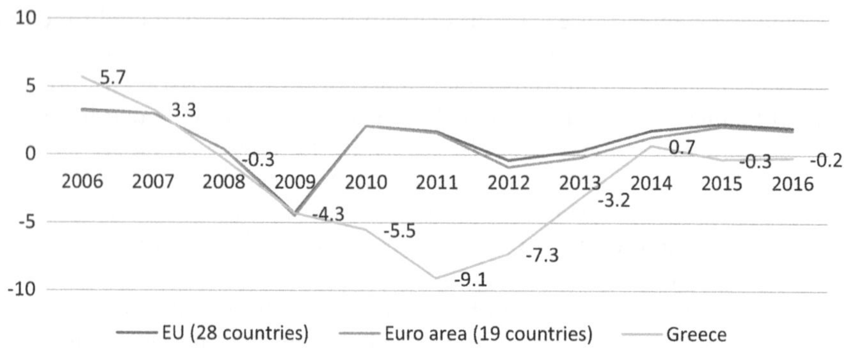

Figure 4.1 Real GDP growth rate – volume (percentage change on previous year).
Source: Eurostat, http://ec.europa.eu/eurostat/tgm/table.do?tab=table&init=1&plugin=1&language=en&pcode=tec00115

Table 4.1 Employment and unemployment in Greece (2006–2016, in thousands)

Year	*Employment*	*Unemployment*	*Average unemployment (per cent)*
2006	4.527,5	448,2	8.9
2007	4.564,1	418,4	8.3
2008	4.610,5	387,9	7.7
2009	4.556,0	484,7	9.5
2010	4.389,8	639,4	12.6
2011	4.054,4	881,8	17.7
2012	3.695,0	1.195,1	24.3
2013	3.513,2	1.330,4	27.2
2014	3.527,0	1.269,6	26.5
2015	3.594,7	1.196,7	25.0
2016	3.658,9	1.126,1	23.0

Source: Own calculation based on data from Hellenic Statistical Authority (ELSTAT).

economic crisis and the policies implemented. The decrease in disposable income in combination with increasing uncertainty resulted in the decrease in almost all forms of economic activity which led to the reduction of total employment. Due to the employment reduction, the ratio of the total number of employees that belong to the working age population aged 15–64 was in 2016 52.2 per cent, almost 11 per cent lower than that for 2008 which stood then at around 63 per cent (Ioannidis, 2013; Karamanis and Hyz, 2014).

The Greek unemployment rate reached its minimum of 7.7 per cent in 2008. However, the unemployment rate has been increasing exponentially since the beginning of the crisis, reaching the worst value in 2013 (27.2 per cent). This means that the unemployment rate in 2013 was above three and a half times higher than the unemployment rate in 2008 (NILHR, 2012). Therefore, the evolution of the number of unemployed in the last ten years has experienced two distinct trends in parallel to the trends identified for the employment rate. In the first trend, the unemployment rate tends to fall until 2008. The second pattern is represented by a progressive and robust increase of unemployment level. Of course, any discussion of the Greek economy and its labour market will need to consider the presence of high self-employment and a variety of informal activities. The size of the shadow economy and the levels of corruption in Greece have been and still are unusually high concerning other developed OECD countries. The estimated Greek shadow economy is roughly three times the size of the Austrian shadow economy and 1.8 times the size of the German estimates (Bitzenis et al., 2016).

4.4 Trends in Greek banking industry condition

In the adverse macroeconomic conditions of the crisis, the Greek banking industry was radically restructured following a series of consolidation actions, which resulted in the transformation of the domestic banking landscape.

In general, from 2006 to 2016, banks in operation have been reduced through mergers, acquisitions, and resolution from 64 at the beginning of the period to 39 at the end (Gortsos, 2014). Almost all foreign banks with the customer service network have left. The four systemic banks (Piraeus Bank, National Bank of Greece, Eurobank, and Alpha Bank) and Attica Bank cumulatively account for more than 95 per cent of the Greek banking system's assets compared with 67.7 per cent at the end of 2006.

Let us see the evolution in more details. Twelve troubled banks, including two major state-owned banks (Agricultural Bank of Greece [ATE Bank] and TT Hellenic Postbank), were tweaked in 2012–2013. In March 2013, Piraeus Bank merged with a 'good part'[2] of the ATE Bank and absorbed the branches of Cypriot banks to prevent the transmission of the Cyprus crisis to Greece,[3] Millennium Bank SA (MBG), Hellenic Bank, and Geniki Bank. The National Bank of Greece has incorporated the sound business of First Business Bank and Probank as well as the deposits of three cooperative banks. Alpha Bank has incorporated Emporiki Bank and Citibank (retail business in Greece). Eurobank has incorporated the Hellenic Postbank, new Proton Bank, and the new TT Bank. In April 2013, Eurobank was nationalised (albeit on a temporary basis) following a failed attempt to merge with the National Bank of Greece. Of all the credit institutions that have their headquarters in Greece, four have been described as systemic for the national economy: National Bank, Piraeus Bank, Alpha Bank, and Eurobank. The concept of 'systemic institution' derives from systemic risk, that is, the risk that can affect the values of a wide range of investments and cannot be avoided through diversification (Kaufmann, 1995). These four banks now account for 90 per cent of total assets (compared to 67.7 per cent in 2006), 95 per cent of deposits, and 95 per cent of the Greek banking system lending.

As at the end of 2016, the Greek banking sector consists of 39 credit institutions with 2,210 branches and 41,211 employees (Bank of Greece, 2017). As the number of credit institutions operating in Greece has been reduced, the degree of concentration has increased considerably. There were four main categories of credit institutions operating in Greece: (1) commercial banks incorporated in Greece and operating under a licence by the Bank of Greece, (2) local cooperative banks incorporated in Greece and operating under a licence by the Bank of Greece, (3) the branches of credit institutions incorporated in the other EU Member States, and (4) the branches of credit institutions incorporated in third countries (outside the EU). Eighteen credit institutions were based in Greece; 17 are branches of commercial banks based in other EU Member States and another 4 are branches of banks based outside the EU, one of which is Bank of America. Among credit institutions which are based in Greece, there are eight commercial banks, nine local cooperative banks, and one Loan and Consignment Fund. The Greek-owned banks cover about 80 per cent of total asset value, foreign-owned banks hold 12 per cent, and the remaining 8 per cent is shared between specialised institutions and local cooperative banks. Comparing to 2006, the number of credit institutions in Greece decreased by almost 70 per cent. The number of bank employees has been reduced by 40 per cent, mainly using voluntary redundancy schemes. The number of bank branches has declined by 42 per cent (Figure 4.2).

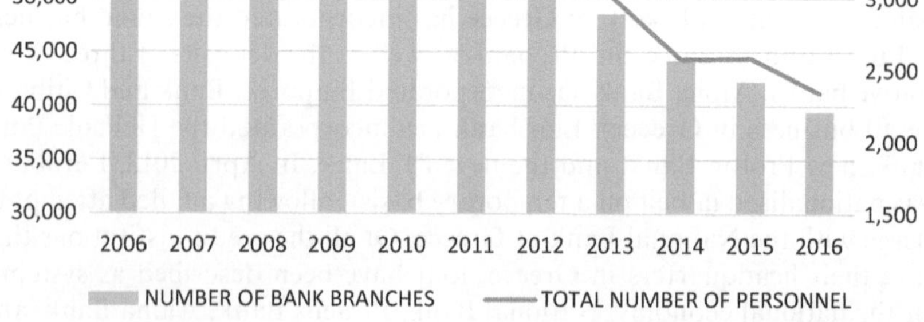

Figure 4.2 The number of bank branches and the total number of personnel in Greek banks, 2006–2016.

Source: Based on data from the Hellenic Bank Association (HBA), 2018.

*This figure shows total number of personnel shown as black line on the left hand and total number of bank branches shown as bars on the right hand.

The larger than initially expected duration and depth of the economic downturn in Greece with very high levels of unemployment, a significant fall in productive activity, a reduction in consumption, and the outflow of deposits created challenging operating conditions for banking institutions (Figure 4.3). During the crisis, the assets of Greek commercial banks declined, according to the data published by the Bank of Greece, by € 114 billion.

Figure 4.4 shows the nominal euro values of total assets for all Greek banks. From 2006 to 2009, total assets almost doubled from € 284.2 billion to € 537.7.

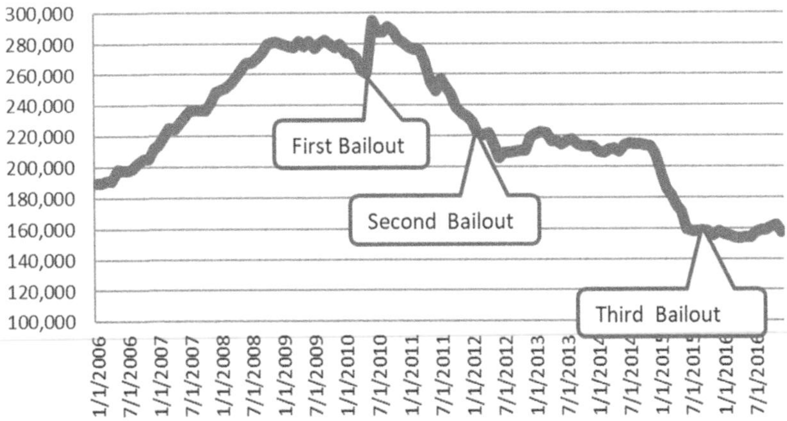

Figure 4.3 Deposits in the Greek Banking System (billion Euro).
Source: Bank of Greece (2018).

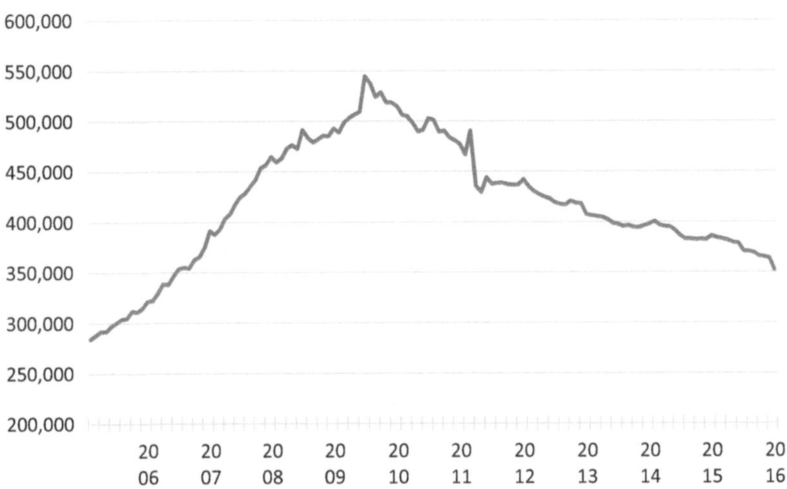

Figure 4.4 Value of total assets.
Source: Bank of Greece (2018).

Clearly evident is rapid asset reduction beginning in 2009. In 2016, the total banks' assets dropped by 35 per cent compared to 2009 and their value was only about 25 per cent higher than in 2006. The drop was especially sharp during the period 2011–2012.

In order to strengthen capital adequacy, Greek banks have raised funds from the Hellenic Financial Stability Fund (HFSF),[4] which was set up in July 2010 to maintain the stability of the Greek banking system.

When eurozone banks face liquidity problems, they look for loans on the interbank market as a first solution or, if this is not feasible due to their lower solvency, they resort to the European Central Bank. For the European Central Bank to lend a bank calls for high-quality guarantees such as government bonds. If funding through Exchange Stabilization Fund is not feasible, for example, due to the low quality of the guarantees provided, the bank is forced to resort to the Emergency Liquidity Assistance (ELA) mechanism. Greek banks have used the liquidity facility since 2012. The imposition of capital controls in June 2015 and the ever-increasing uncertainty led to a further decline in the confidence of savers and the liquidity of Greek banks.

Figure 4.5 shows data for the ratio of the book value of bank equity capital, loans, and provisions for bad loan expressed as a percentage of total bank assets aggregate for Greek banks during 2006–2016. By these indicators, banking conditions were noticeably stronger before the recent financial crisis. During the period 2007 and mid-2009, loan ratio was lower than during the next few years. Starting from 2010, provisions for bad loans rose so did the equity ratio after the crunch of 2011. During the reviewed period, the most

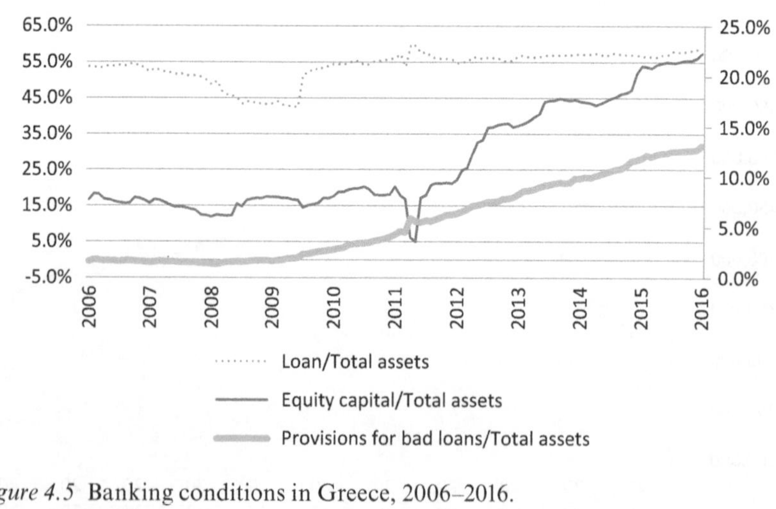

Figure 4.5 Banking conditions in Greece, 2006–2016.
Source: Bank of Greece (2018).

*This figure shows ratio of book value of bank equity to total banks assets shown as black line on the right hand, provisions for bad loans to total assets shown as the bold, black line on the right hand, and loan to total assets ratio shown as black round dot line on the left hand.

essential changes in assets structure were as follows: (a) despite declining in absolute terms, loans were almost stable as a percentage of total assets, due to the above-mentioned fall in total assets, and (b) equity capital as a percentage of total assets increased after its sharp reduction at the end of 2011.

4.5 Capital controls and its impact on banks' operation

In 2015, capital restrictions were imposed in Greece due to the Greek government's inability to reach an agreement with its lenders. Negative results of the five-month negotiations with the members of Eurogroup culminated in early elections in January 2015 and the establishment of a coalition government of two parties: Coalition of the Radical Left (Syriza) and Independent Greeks (Anel). New negotiation began with the logic of debt cancellation and country disengagement from the memorandums, but the attitude of the country's partners was insurmountable on these issues, leading to a waste of time and expectations. During this time, the Greek banks declined sharply, leading to strong concern about the ability to maintain the country's liquidity and the viability of Greek banks. On Friday, June 26, 2015, the country's prime minister announced a referendum on July 5, in response to the ensuing set-up of partners to accept their proposal within the day. Following the above events, the European Central Bank decided not to further increase the level of its ELA for Greek banks. In June 2015, capital controls were introduced. As a result, the Greek government was forced to close Greek banks for almost 20 days immediately and to implement controls on bank transfers from Greek banks to foreign banks and limits on cash withdrawals to avoid an uncontrolled bank run and a complete collapse of the Greek banking system (Samitas and Polyzos, 2016). Cash withdrawal per customer was limited to the amount of € 60 per day or € 420 per week cumulatively, while particular categories of transactions were identified which, after approval, could be circumvented.

According to the Cash Report (2016), Greece has the highest percentage of cash usage in the entire EU. During the last decades, the use of electronic means of payments (EMPs) in Greece lags considerably behind the rest of the EU. Although the growth recorded since 2001, Greece continues to occupy very low positions in the relevant rankings. Based on the value of transactions with EMPs per inhabitant in 2013, Greece ranked higher only compared to Croatia and Bulgaria, while concerning the number of transactions per inhabitant Greece occupied the last position in the ranking (IOBE, 2015; European Central Bank, 2017). In order to reach the EU average for this ranking, the number of EMP transactions per inhabitant in Greece should increase by about 11 times from their 2013 level. Thus, the potential for further growth is significant (IOBE, 2015).

The introduction of capital controls in Greece in the summer of 2015 has led to significant changes in consumers' behaviour. Capital controls have had positive side effects, with the improvement of the banking system's liquidity by curbing the massive deposit outflows and capital flight abroad. The bank holiday, the compulsory acceptance of payment cards, and the daily limit on ATM withdrawals gave a significant boost to the diffusion of digital payments (IOBE, 2015). Both the value and the number of domestic transactions with payment cards issued in Greece more than doubled, month on month, in July 2015 (+103 per cent and +105 per cent, respectively; IOBE, 2015). Some months later and after a partial relaxation of restrictions on capital movements, consumers have continued to increase the use of plastic money. The use of debit cards during the first five months of capital controls increased by 40 per cent, while the credit cards use increased by about 10 per cent. In 2016, credit card payments in Greece reached a total value of approximately € 4.9 billion.[5] Small Enterprises' Institute of the Hellenic Confederation of Professionals, Craftsmen and Merchants' survey (IME GSEVEE, 2017) showed an increase in POS use of 20 per cent within one year of the implementation of capital restrictions. According to this research, from January 2016 to January 2017, we observe an increase in the number of cards transactions by 1.345 per cent, increase in the value of card payments by 136 per cent, the number of installed POS terminals in Greece reached 600,000 in January 2017, and debit cards are 81 per cent of the total number of active cards in circulation (11.8 million), with 1.3 million issued in 2015–2016. A large increase of the demand for POS terminals was caused by Greece's Law 4446/2016 amended the country's tax system providing for a person's tax-exempt income to be linked to the minimal value of spending via electronic means (KPMG, 2017). This law was put in force from the beginning of 2017, and according to it what is deemed tax-free income is linked to a minimum value of expenses that a taxpayer incurs, provided that payment be affected by electronic means, depending on the individuals' level of income. A progressive scale was applied for the determination of the income tax reduction related to electronic transactions. The measure was aimed at tax compliance of people in business and creating a culture of use of plastic money by citizens. After the introduction of this law, applications for POS systems from Greek firms doubled reaching 8,000 per month. At the same time, about 80 per cent of retail sales were realised through the POS system.

Finally, paragraph 3 of Article 20 of Law 3842/2010, as amended by paragraph 2 of Article 69 of Law 4446/2016, stipulated that from December 22, 2015, onwards the trading threshold would be reduced from € 1,500 to € 500, above which transactions between individuals and businesses (for the sale of goods or the provision of services) should be carried out exclusively through the use of card-based payment instruments or other EMP (as, for instance, electronic funds transfer, use of an electronic wallet).

As part of the measures taken to reduce withdrawals, the representatives of four systemic Greek banks proposed to the government to implement extra tax on cash withdrawals in order to boost the use of plastic money. The aim of the banks was the creation of disincentives, in order to make cash use unprofitable.

In the context of combating tax evasion and the need for an increase of e-payments, the Ministry of Finance proceeded with the decision to mandatorily install POS terminals by specific professional sectors related with high tax evasion.

With the imposition of the bank holiday during the summer of 2015 and the capital controls after, the use of EMP recorded remarkable growth rates. However, even with the sharp increase that was observed under the extraordinary circumstances, the position of Greece in the rankings did not improve much due to the large gap from most other EU countries. The maintenance of capital controls negatively affects macroeconomic aggregates, while their elimination crucially hinges on economic developments and the restoration of depositors' confidence.

4.6 CAMELS rating system

The recent crisis has had a significant impact on the Greek banking sector and the soundness of individual banks. The ongoing global financial turbulence in Greece has highlighted the importance of early identification of weak banks. The commercial banks' risks come from all the uncertainty of the banking business, which has infusibility and hidden features, if not timely controlled will have a negative impact on the national economy. In this section, the Uniform Financial Rating System, known as the CAMELS rating system, will be used to determine a bank's overall condition, its safety and soundness, and to identify its strengths and weaknesses (financial, operational, and managerial), and its potential risks which may lead to bank failure. This rating ensures a bank's healthy conditions by reviewing different aspects of a bank based on a variety of information sources such as a financial statement, funding sources, and cash flow. The six factors are represented by the acronym 'CAMELS', where C stands for capital adequacy, A for asset quality, M for management capability/soundness, E for earnings and profitability, L for liquidity, and S for sensitivity to market risk. The choice of the six factors is based on the idea that each represents a significant aspect of banking (Mayes and Stremmel, 2012). Main key consideration and main ratios in each factor are:

1 Capital adequacy is focused on the composition and trends of a bank's capital and tries to evaluate if a bank is capitalised appropriately, what are the characteristics of a bank's debt, and how much of a bank's net assets are unrestricted (Mayes and Stremmel, 2012). In other words, it is capital expected to maintain balance with the risk's exposure of the financial institution such as credit risk, market risk, and operational risk, in order to absorb the potential losses and protect the financial institution's debt holder. As critical ratios for the evaluation of the capital adequacy, we may use growth in assets and net assets, capital/deposit ratio, capital-risk asset ratio, average lending capital interest rate,

leverage ratios, capital adequacy ratio (CAR) capital to risk-weighted assets ratio, the ratio of capital to assets, and so on.

2 Asset quality is focused on loan portfolio strength and considers the composition of the loan portfolio, type and amount of collateral, loan policies, and processes. Measuring the asset quality is quite difficult. The asset quality indicators highlight the use of NPLs ratios, which are the allowance or provision to loan losses reserve. For the evaluation of asset quality, we may use NPLs to total loans, NPLs to total equity, provision for loan loss ratio, loan loss reserve ratio, annual net charge-off ratio, and portfolio at risk.
3 Management capability or quality with a focus on the ability of management to identify, measure, guide, and control the organisation. It is one of the most critical elements of a rating system, since the management plays a substantial role in a bank's success. Leading indicators are total assets growth rate, loan growth rate, and earnings growth rate.
4 Bank's earnings and profitability are focused on the level, diversification and sustainability of bank's income sources, the ability of the bank to control costs, and management of net interest margins. Profitability ratios measure the ability of a company to generate profits from revenue and assets. One of the most general ratios which may be used is income ratio measure as total revenue to total expenses, return on assets (ROA), return on equity (ROE), and net interest income ratio.
5 The liquidity expresses the degree to which a bank is capable of fulfilling its respective obligations. Liquidity refers to the sufficient levels of operating cash and lending capital available to operate without interruption and may be measured by the ratio of total loan to customer deposits and customer deposits to total assets.
6 Sensitivity measures the impact on the bank's portfolio due to future market changes and may be measured by the portfolio concentration risk.

4.6.1 Data sets and methodology

There is no uniform way of deciding on which indicators to be included to measure each of the aspects (Hyz and Gikas, 2016). The indicators to proxy the CAMELS dimensions are as follows:

1 CAR for Capital Adequacy: Higher CAR ratio indicates stronger bank and bigger protection of investors. It is expressed as a percentage of a bank's risk-weighted credit exposures. Tier One Capital can absorb losses without a bank being required to cease trading and Tier Two Capital can absorb losses in the event of a winding-up and so provides a lesser degree of protection to depositors.

$$CAR = \frac{Tier\ One\ Capital + Tier\ Two\ Capital}{Risk\ Weighted\ Assets} \tag{4.1}$$

2 Net Non-performing Assets Ratio (NPA) for Asset Quality: Due to the widespread of banks' activities and the range of assets figures disclosed, there is a wide variety of potential indicators. Since the dominating business of commercial banks is lending, it is reasonable to focus on this asset group. An NPA are those assets for which interest is overdue for more than 90 days. Higher ratio reflects the rising bad quality of loans.

$$NPA\ ratio = \frac{Net\ non-performing\ assets}{Loans\ given} \tag{4.2}$$

3 Overhead Expenses to Net Operating Revenues for Management Quality: Lower values of this indicator suggest better management quality. The measure of management quality is one of the most complicated aspects of every company is trying to reflect the board of directors' and management's ability to identify, measure, monitor, and control the risks of the activities (Uniform Financial Institutions Rating System, 1997, p. 6).

$$ER = \frac{Overhead\ Expenses}{Net\ Operating\ Revenues} \tag{4.3}$$

4 ROA and ROE for Earnings: ROA ratio is the net income (profit) generated by the bank on its total assets. The higher the proportion of average earnings assets, the better would be the resulting returns on total assets. Similarly, ROE indicates returns earned by the bank on its total net worth.

$$ROA = \frac{Net\ profits}{Avg.\ total\ assets} \tag{4.4}$$

$$ROE = \frac{Net\ profits}{Avg.\ total\ net\ worth} \tag{4.5}$$

5 Current Assets to Total Assets Ratio and Total Loans to Total Customers Deposits for Liquidity:

$$Current\ Assets\ to\ Total\ Assets = \frac{Current\ Assets}{Average\ Total\ assets} \tag{4.6}$$

$$Loan\ to\ Deposit\ Ratio = \frac{Total\ loans}{Total\ customers\ deposits} \tag{4.7}$$

6 Total Volatile Liabilities to Total Assets for Sensitivity to Market Risk: The concern is with the impact on banks from shifts and fluctuations in the financial market.

$$Volatile\ Liabilities\ Ratio = \frac{Total\ volatile\ liabilities}{Total\ Assets} \tag{4.8}$$

In the next step, we assigned each bank a score on a scale of one (best) to five (worst) for each factor. In the context, for example, of capital adequacy, a rating of one indicates a strong capital level relative to the financial institution's risk. Meanwhile, the rating of five indicates a critical deficient level of capital in which immediate assistance from shareholders or external resources is required. Later, we computed the weighted average CAMELS rating score. To compute the weighted average CAMELS rating score, we used the CAMELS rating components, according to Final Rules of Large Bank Pricing, with the following standard weights: Capital Adequacy 20 per cent, Asset Quality 20 per cent, Management 20 per cent, Earnings 10 per cent, Liquidity 20 per cent, and Sensitivity to market risk 10 per cent. As a result, the CAMELS Ratio is obtained as follows:

$$\begin{aligned} CAMELS = {} & 0{,}20 * CAR + 0{,}20 * A + 0{,}20 * M + 0{,}10 * (ROA + ROE)/2 \\ & + 0{,}20(L1 + L2)/2 + 0{,}10 * S \end{aligned} \tag{4.9}$$

We can distinguish five main categories of ratings:

1 Range 1.00–1.49 – 'strong' or 'outstanding'.
2 Range 1.50–2.49 – 'satisfactory' or 'superior'.
3 Range 2.50–3.49 – 'fair' or 'average'.
4 Range 3.50–4.49 – 'marginal' or 'underperform'.
5 Range 4.50–5.00 – 'unsatisfactory' or 'doubtful'.

In general, CAMELS rating is integer ratings that vary from one (best rating) to five (worst rating), and if a bank has an average score less than two, it is considered to be a high-quality institution, while banks with scores higher than three are considered to be less-than-satisfactory establishments. The institutions with grade four and five are rated to be insolvent. The system helps to identify banks that need supervisory attention.

The starting point for the analysis were the data extracted from the ICAP database, containing detailed financial reports annuals (income statements and annuals balance sheets) and statistics on Greek companies. The study covered the abovementioned four biggest Greek banks, namely, Alpha Bank, Eurobank, National Bank of Greece, and Piraeus Bank. The observation period starts in 2006 and ends in 2016. In the analysis, we used the CAMELS Rating System, which is used by bank supervisory authorities' rate institutions.

4.6.2 Implementation of CAMELS system rating – the results

This section presents the results of the implementation of the CAMELS system rating for four main Greek banks during the period 2006–2016

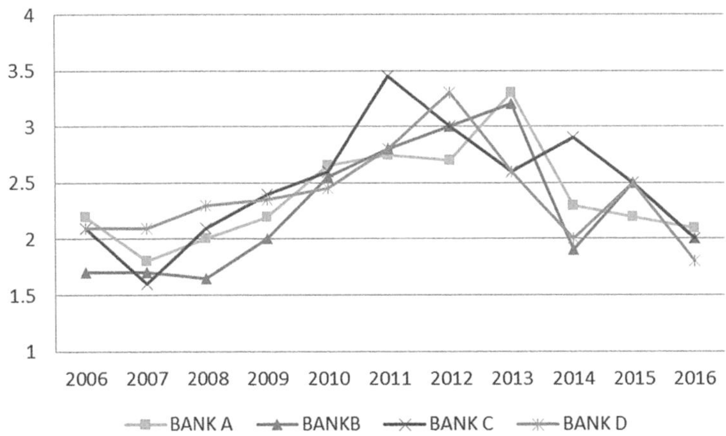

Figure 4.6 Results of system rating analysis.
Source: Own calculations.

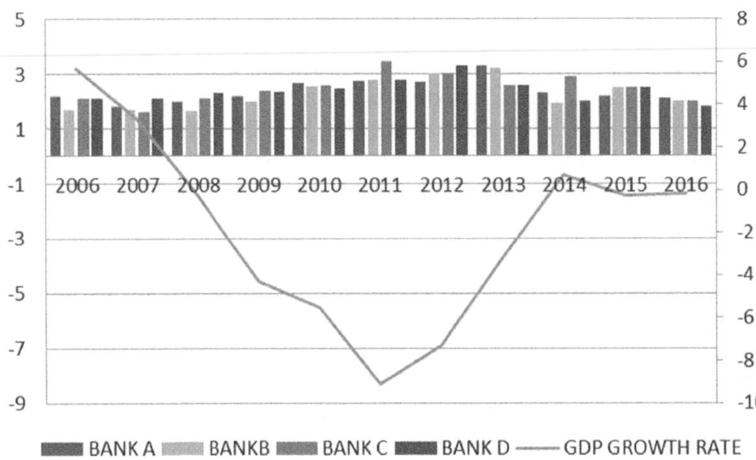

Figure 4.7 Greek GDP and CAMELS.
Source: Own calculations.

*This figure shows CAMELS results for Greek systemic banks shown as bars on the left hand and GDP growth rate shown as black line on the right hand.

(Figures 4.6 and 4.7). Due to the confidentiality of banks data used in the analyses, we are not revealing the name of the investigated bank. Instead, we call the banks as Bank A, B, C, and D. In the US, where the National Credit Union Administration adopts CAMELS rating from 1987, a bank's rating is highly confidential and never made public, even on a lagged basis (Hirtle and Lopez, 1999).

Based on the results of our research, the key developments during the financial years 2006–2016 were:

1 During the examined period, the situation of four surveyed banks worsened. CAMELS indicator achieved a maximum value in 2008 in the case of Bank B (1,65) and the lowest in 2011 in the case of Bank C (3,45). The highest range for the entire period was Bank C. After steadily deteriorating till 2013, the minimum improvement was recorded.
2 The situation of the surveyed four banks according to CAMELS methodology can be described as 'satisfactory' to 'fair', with the tendency after 2011 to increasing the share of 'less-than-satisfactory' institutions (a score greater than three).
3 Greek domestic banks during the period under investigation were among Europe's most robust concerning capital adequacy with CAR standing at 11 per cent and over.
4 The main problem is the bank's Assets Quality measure by NPA. The Greek banks have to review the troubled assets, assessment of NPL management policies, restructuring NPLs to increase revenues and recoverability, and estimate the expected loss under different scenarios. A strong capital base is necessary for banks to get non-performing loans under control. The NPLs were mainly due to the portion of outstanding consumer loans, which has displayed a rapid growth rate over the past three crisis years, hitting 43.8 per cent by mid-2013. Higher NPL ratios are directly correlated with the increase in the unemployment rate as the intensification of the Greek labour market crisis impacts borrowers' ability to service their loans.
5 The other major challenge for the credit sector, which will also determine the declining rate of bad loans, is the return to an increase in the issue of loans. The sooner Greece achieves this return to credit expansion, the sooner bad loans will begin to drop.
6 On the cost front (factor 'Management'), synergies stemming from recent acquisitions should drive expenses down. These positive trends are expected to improve efficiency through the coming years.
7 The situation of the Greek bank was correlated with the whole economic situation. As the Greek GDP decreased during the years of crisis, CAMELS indicators worsened despite the efforts of governments to strengthen the banking sector. The future of Greek banking sector depends mostly on political, economic stability, and on the efforts to strengthen the real economy.

4.6.3 Non-performing exposures of the Greek commercial banks by portfolio

As a result of the general economic and political situation in Greece, Greek banks' ratios of bad loans remained over 45.2 per cent (€ 107.6 billion) on their total loan portfolio and was the highest in Europe.

Table 4.2 Structure of total exposures and non-performing exposures of the Greek commercial banks by portfolio

Total exposures		*From which:*				
		Business				*Retail*
€ 240.3 billion		*€ 145.5 billion (44.7 per cent)*				*€ 94.8 billion (45.7 per cent)*
From which:		*Large corporates*	*SMEs*	*Small business and professionals*	*Other business activities*	
		€ 51 billion (29.1 per cent)	*€ 39.2 billion (59.9 per cent)*	*€ 25 billion (67.2 per cent)*	*€ 30.4 billion (33.1 per cent)*	
Unlikely to pay	28 per cent	45 per cent	26 per cent	15 per cent	45 per cent	23 per cent
>90 dpd (exl. Denounced)	28 per cent	26 per cent	26 per cent	30 per cent	37 per cent	28 per cent
Denounced exposures	44 per cent	29 per cent	48 per cent	55 per cent	19 per cent	49 per cent

Source: Bank of Greece, 2018.

At the end of 2016, the total exposures reached € 240.3 billion; 44 per cent (€ 105.7 million) constituted denounced exposure,[6] 28 per cent unlikely to pay that are not past due or past due $\leq$90 dpd[7] (€ 67.3 million), and also exposures in arrears above 90 dpt excluding denounced loans[8] constituted 28 per cent. The highest ratios are observed in sole proprietorships (67.2 per cent) and small and medium-sized enterprises (59.9 per cent) as far as the business portfolio is considered and consumer (55.3 per cent) and residential (41.8 per cent) in the retail portfolio (Table 4.2). Effectively managing the stock of NPEs by streamlining the insolvency framework and taking further measures to resolve NPEs are crucial for achieving sustainable growth over the long term.

Notes

1 The H-statistic is calculated by summing the estimated elasticities of revenue to factor prices, with a value of one indicating perfect competition, a value of zero (or less) indicating monopoly, and intermediate values indicating the degree of monopolistic competition.
2 Selected assets and liabilities.
3 Bank of Cyprus and Cyprus Popular Bank in Greece.
4 The HFSF was established in 2010 by Law 3864/2010 as a legal person of private law with a capital of € 50 billion from the financial support mechanism for the Greek economy by eurozone Member States, the European Central Bank, and the International Monetary Fund. At the end of the first round of recapitalisation, HFSF became the dominant shareholder, although with restricted voting rights, controlling an 81 per cent stake in Piraeus Bank, and 84 per cent in Alpha and National, HFSF stake in Eurobank was 95.2 per cent with full voting

rights. The four banks subsequently proceeded with capital increases, in which HFSF did not participate. Since the HFSF did not participate in recent capital increases, its share in the banks' capital was diluted to an average of around 60 per cent. More specifically, HFSF's current participation in Eurobank stands at 35.4 per cent (with restricted voting rights), in NBG at 57.2 per cent, in Piraeus at 67.3 per cent, and in Alpha at 69.9 per cent.

5 www.statista.com/markets/414/topic/459/banks-financial-services/

6 Denounced Loans are loans which their contract has been called on the lender and the denouncement has adequately been announced to the debtor.

7 Subcategory of exposures unlikely to pay were deemed as non-performing, even though they were either under current status or under past due up to 90 days status (EBA, Annex V. Part 2, 159).

8 Exposures in arrears, above 90 dpd, excluding denounced loans, present the subcategory of exposures that are in arrears status, above 90 dpd.

References

Abbasoglu, O.F, Aysan, A.F., Gunes, A., 2007, Concentration, competition, efficiency and profitability of the Turkish Banking Sector in the post-crises period, *Banks and Bank Systems*, Vol. 2, No. 3, pp. 106–115.

Anderson, J.E., 1999, Making operational sense of mergers and acquisitions, *The Electricity Journal*, Vol. 12, No. 7, pp. 49–59.

Bank of Greece, 2017, Overview of the Greek Financial System, Bank of Greece, Eurosystem.

Berger, A.N., Hannan, T., 1989, The price-concentration relationship in banking, *The Review of Economics and Statistics*, Vol. 71, No. 2, pp. 291–299.

Bertoncelj, A., Kovac, D., 2007, An integrated approach for a higher success rate in mergers and acquisitions, *Proceedings of Rijeka Faculty of Economics: Journal of Economics & Business*, Vol. 25, No. 1, pp. 167–188.

Bikker, J.A., 2004, *Competition and Efficiency in a Unified European Banking Market*, Edward Elgar Publishing Limited: Cheltenham & Northampton, MA.

Bikker, J.A., Bos, J.W., 2004, *Trends in Competition and Profitability in the Banking Industry: A Basic Framework*, Vol. 18, SUERF Studies 2005/2.

Bitzenis, A., Vlachos, V., Schneider, F., 2016, An exploration of the Greek shadow economy: Can its transfer into the official economy provide economic relief amid the crisis? *Journal of Economic Issue*, Vol. 50, No. 1, pp. 165–196.

Carletti, E., Hartmann, P., 2002, *Competition and Stability: What's Special about Banking?* May 2002, Working Paper No. 146, European Central Bank.

Cartwright, S., Cooper, C.L., 1994, The human effects of mergers and acquisitions, in Cooper, C.L., Rousseau, D.M., eds., *Trends in Organisational Behaviour*, John Wiley and Sons: New York.

Cartwright, S., Schoenberg, R., 2006, Thirty years of mergers and acquisitions research: Recent advances and future opportunities, *British Journal of Management*, Vol. 17, No. 1, pp. 11–18.

Chambers, K., Honeycutt, A., 2009, Telecommunications mega-mergers: Impact on employee morale and turnover intention, *Journal of Business and Economic Research*, Vol. 7, No. 2, February, pp. 77–93.

Claessens, S., Laeven, L., 2003, What drives bank competition? Some international evidence, *Policy Research Working Paper Series*, No. 3113, The World Bank.

DePamphilis, D., 2008, *Mergers, Acquisitions, and Other Restructuring Activities*, Elsevier, Academic Press: New York.

Egli, D., Rime, B., 1999, The UBS-SBC merger and competition in the Swiss retail banking sector, *Studienzentrum Gerzensee Working Paper*, No. 2, December.

European Central Bank, 2017, *The Use of Cash by Households in the Euro Area*, G4S, Cash Report Europe.

Gaston–Gelos, R., Roldos, J., 2002, *Consolidation and Market Structure in Emerging Market Banking System*, IMF Working Paper, WP/ 02/186.

Gortsos, Ch., 2014, *The Impact of the Current Eurozone Fiscal Crisis on the Greek Banking System*, retrieved from http://gr2014.eu/sites/default/files/C.Gortsos%20-%20greek%20banking%20system%20fiscal%20crisis.pdf

Gutiérrez de Rozas, L., 2007, Testing for competition in the Spanish Banking Industry: The Panzar-Rosse approach revisited, Banco de España, *Research Paper* No. WP-0726, August.

Hempell, H.S., 2002, Testing for competition among German Banks, *Discussion Paper 04/02*, Economic Research Centre of the Deutsche Bundesbank.

Hirschman, A.O., 1964, The paternity of an index, *The American Economic Review*, Vol. 54, No. 5, p. 761.

Hirtle, B., Lopez, J.A., 1999, Supervisory information and the frequency of bank examination, Federal Reserve Bank of New York, *Economic Policy Review*, Vol. 5, No. 1, April, pp. 1–20.

Hunsaker, P.L., Coombs. M.W., 1988, Mergers and acquisitions. Managing the emotional issues, *Personnel Journal*, Vol. 67, No. 2, pp. 56–78.

Hyz, A., 2009, Consolidation process in polish banking sector – cultural aspects, *Review of Economic Sciences*, Discussion Papers, Vol. 3, No. 2, pp. 1–23.

Hyz, A., 2011, Issues in consolidation and competition: Case of polish banking sector, *International Journal of Humanities and Social Science*, Vol. 1, No. 8, July, pp. 5–18.

Hyz, A., Gikas, G., 2016, CAMELS and Greek banking sector performance during the crisis. An analysis and review of the evidence, *Acta Universitatis Lodziensis, Folia Oeconomica*, Vol. 5, No. 316, pp. 12–28.

IME GSEVEE Survey, 2017, Biannual representation of economic climate trends, February 2017, retrieved on 21/08/2018 from http://www.imegsevee.gr/pressrelease/1085-ime-gsevee-survey-february - 2017-biannual-representation-of-economic-climate-in-small-enterprises-

Ioannidis, Y., 2013, *Hidden Unemployment in Greece*, Paper No. 52120, Munich Personal RePEc Archive (MPRA) Munich.

IOBE (Foundation for Economic and Industrial Research), 2015, *Digital payments and tax revenues in Greece*, retrieved on 12/05/2017 from http://iobe.gr/research_dtl_en.asp?RID=162

Karamanis, K., Hyz, A., 2014, Flexible working and unemployment in Greece: An analysis and review of the evidence, *International Journal of Academic Research in Business and Social Sciences*, Vol. 4, No. 10, October, pp. 123–167.

Kaufman, G., 1995, Comment on systemic risk, in Kaufman, G. ed., *Research in Financial Services*, Vol. 7, Greenwich: JAI Press, pp. 47–52.

Kenneth, D.J., Critchfield, T., 2005, Consolidation in the U.S. Banking Industry: Is the “Long, Strange Trip” about to end? *Federal Deposit Insurance Corporation Banking Review*, Vol. 17, No. 4, pp. 1–23.

King, R., Levine, E., 1993, Finance, entrepreneurship and growth: theory and evidence, *Journal of Monetary Economics*, Vol. 32, No. 3, December, pp. 513–542.

Koutsomanoli-Fillipaki, N., Staikouras, Ch., 2004, *Competition and concentration in the New European banking Landscape*, Department of Accounting and Finance, Athens University of Economics and Business, Greece.

KPMG, 2017, Greece – New Law Amends Income Tax System, retrieved on 12/06/2017 from https://home.kpmg.com/xx/en/home/insights/2017/04/flash-alert-2017-073.html

Levine, R., 1997, Financial development and economic growth, *Journal of Economic Literature*, Vol. 35, No. 2, pp. 688–726.

Levine, R., Zervos, S., 1998, Stock markets, banks, and economic growth, *The American Economic Review*, Vol. 88, No. 3, pp. 537–558.

Mayes, D.G., Stremmel, H., 2012, *The Effectiveness of Capital Adequacy Measures in Predicting Bank, Distress*, retrieved on 10/08/2018 from www.rbnz.govt.nz/research_and_publications/seminars_and_workshops/dec2012/Session3_Mayes.162502.pdf

Neviana, S., 2003, Effects of Consolidation in Italian Banking Local Markets, Clusters, Industrial Districts and Firms: The Challenge of Globalization. *Conference in honour of Professor Sebastiano Brusco,* Modena, Italy, September 12–13, 2003.

NILHR, 2012, *National Institute of Labour and Human Resources, Labour and Employment in Greece*, Annual Report, 2012, Athens.

Northcott, C.A., 2004, *Competition in Banking: The Review of the Literature*, Working Paper 2004, No. 24, Bank of Canada.

Panzar, J.C., Rosse, J.N., 1987, Testing for monopoly equilibrium, *Journal of Industrial Economics*, Vol. 1, No. 35, pp. 443–456.

Pikula, D.A., 2008, *Mergers & Acquisitions: Organizational Culture & HR Issues*, Industrial Relations Centre, Queen's University, Kingston.

Prager, R.A., Hannan, T.H., 1998, The relaxation of entry barriers in the banking industry: an empirical investigation, *Journal of Financial Services Research*, Vol. 14, No. 3, pp. 171–188.

Prasad, A., Ghosh, E., 2005, Competition in Indian banking, *IMF Working Paper*, No. WP/05/141.

Romanyuk, Y., 2010, *Asset – Liability Management: An Overview*, Discussion Paper, Bank of Canada, No. 10, 2010.

Rosenbaum, J., Joshua, P., 2009, *Investment Banking: Valuation, Leveraged Buyouts, and Mergers & Acquisitions*, John Wiley & Sons: Hoboken, NJ.

Samitas, A., Polyzos, S., 2016, Freeing Greece from capital controls: were the restrictions enforced in time? *Research in International Business and Finance*, Vol. 37, No. 3, pp. 34–45.

Sapienza, P., 2002, The effect of Banking mergers on loan contracts, *Journal of Finance*, Vol. 57, No. 1, pp. 329–368.

Shull, B., Hanweck, G.A., 2001, *Bank Mergers in a Deregulated Environment: Promise and Peril*, Quorum Books: Westport, CT.

Strahan, P.E., Weston, J., 1996, Small business lending and bank consolidation: is there cause for concern? *Economic and Finance*, Federal Reserve Bank of New York, Vol. 2, pp. 1–6.

Strahan, P.E., Weston, J., 1998, Small business lending and the changing structure of the banking industry, *Journal of Banking and Finance*, Vol. 22, pp. 821–845.

Sudarsanam, S., 2003, *Creating value from mergers and acquisitions: the challenges, an international and integrated perspective*, FT Prentice Hall International UK.

Uniform Financial Institutions Rating System, 1997, Federal Register, Vol. 62, No. 3, retrieved on 17/7/2018 from https://www.govinfo.gov/content/pkg/FR-1997-01-06/pdf/97-155.pdf

Walraven, N., 1997, Small business lending by banks involved in mergers, *Finance and Economics Discussion Series*, 97–25, Board of Governors of the Federal Reserve.

Wiley, A.N., 2004, *Mergers and Acquisitions: Managing the HR Issues*, retrieved on 12/04/2018 from http://icmr.icfai.org/casestudies/mergerissues1.htm

Yeyati, E.L., Micco, A., 2007, Concentration and foreign penetration in Latin American banking sectors: impact on competition and risk, *Journal of Banking & Finance*, Elsevier, Vol. 31, No. 6, pp. 1633–1647.

Yildirim, H.S., Philippatos, G.C., 2007, Restructuring, consolidation and competition in Latin American banking markets, *Journal of Banking and Finance*, Vol. 31, No. 3, pp. 34–47.

Zardkoohi, A., Kolari, J., 1997, *The Effect of Structural Changes in the US Banking Industry on Small Business Lending*, Working Paper, Texas A&M University.

Zawalinska, K., 1999, *Asset and Liability Management. The Institutional Approach to ALM by Commercial Banks in Poland: A Special Focus on Risk Management*, Center for Social and Economic Research, Warsaw, 185.

5 State of the business economy

Profitability and dependence on debt

5.1 Introduction

In a country where 85 per cent of private employment is concentrated in SMEs and more than 50 per cent in microenterprises, a prolonged recession exacerbated by austerity measures has profoundly affected Greek companies. According to the international literature (OECD, 2009; Lallement, 2011; Ali, 2012; Berkmen et al., 2012; European Commission, 2012), the economic crisis has resulted in the classification of firms into four categories based on two criteria: financial strength and competitive advantage. Financial strength depends on the ability of an enterprise to continue to operate without direct support from external sources. Thus, companies that do not need immediate external financing are classified as financially strong, while those who need immediate external financing are classified as financially weak (Ernst & Young, 2013) The competitive advantage of a company is determined by whether the performance was better or worse than its competitors in the following five aspects: cost, product position in the market (strong brand name or not), technological capabilities, leadership and management, and ability to influence/cooperate with local authorities. Consequently, firms that performed better than their competitors in three or more of these aspects indicate a highly competitive advantage, while firms that are better in two or fewer dimensions indicate low competitive advantage (OECD, 2009). The four categories of companies are strong companies characterised by the high financial strength and competitive advantage, stable companies that are financially strong but competitively weak, small companies which are economically weak but have a strong competitive advantage, and 'failed' companies that are weak both financially and competitively.

In Greece, it is more imperative than ever to increase the competitiveness of the enterprises, focusing on high expertise and added value. As described in Chapter 2, the productivity and competitiveness of small and medium-sized Greek firms are significantly below the European average. Generally, the combined share of Greek SMEs specialising in high-tech manufacturing and knowledge-intensive services, which are likely to be more productive, is only 18 per cent in Greece, while these SMEs are almost a third of the EU total. Strengthening the capabilities of Greek firms' production, combining the skills of human resources by investing in education and research, may contribute to the development of innovation, productivity, and exports. In the new reality of permanent insecurity, globalisation, and technological changes, as we described in Chapter 1, modern and competitive production knowhow emerging as a key factor enhances the economy's resilience in times of crisis (UNIDO, 2013).

The structure of the Greek economy with a large share of SMEs makes it very sensitive to fluctuations in the business cycle. Small businesses are always hit harder during financial crises because they are more dependent on bank credit to fund their growth. The conditions of credit markets act as a 'financial accelerator' for small firms. When we talk about financial accelerator, we mean the process by which adverse shocks to the economy amplify worsening financial market conditions (Bernanke and Gertler, 1995; Bernanke et al. 1999; Bernanke, 2007). Small firms feel the up- and downswings more acutely due to their reliance on the flow of bank credit.

The financial crisis and the recession negatively affected credit flows to businesses for several reasons. Making a conceptual distinction between supply-side and demand-side factors in credit markets is difficult. On the supply side, there has been a weak financial situation of the banking system, non-performing loans, and insufficient capital which led to the tightening of credit standards for bank loans to non-financial firms. At the same time, borrower-specific situation, also associated with creditworthiness, influenced the demand for loans. On the demand side, the persistently weak level of economic activity, high uncertainty, low confidence, and the need to reduce the debt levels have continued to weigh on borrowing. On the other side, general macroeconomic conditions and the availability of internal financing were also affecting the demand for banks debt.

There is evidence that many parts of the banking sector are still reeling from the financial crisis. Many banks are themselves in trouble, as they suffered from increased loan defaults and had insufficient capital to make loans. The situation in the Greek banking sector during the last few years was characterised by consolidation process and concentration, worsening of the banking sector's financial situation with an increase in the Net Non-performing Assets Ratio, and continuous decrease in deposits by domestic enterprises and households. We have presented the situation in the Greek banking sector in Chapter 4 of this study analytically.

The aim of the present chapter is twofold. First, it attempts to evaluate the profitability and business dependence on debt. Second, it aims to explore the relationship between determinants which are specific for firms and their capital structure. With this in mind, we collected a panel of 612 SMEs covering the period 2006–2016. The study of the determinants of capital structure of SMEs usually relates to large and listed companies. Even though SMEs constitute the most predominant type of companies in Greece, these companies have traditionally been given little attention in financial research in general and in Greece notably.

5.2 Data sources

Trying to analyse the situation of the business economy in Greece, we use data from the small and medium-sized sector of the Epirus region in Greece. There are three data sources used in this research. Financial data were extracted from the ICAP database, containing detailed annual financial reports of Greek companies (income statements and annual balance sheets). Complementary data were collected from the Chambers of Epirus and the national statistics on Greek companies.

The criteria used for selection of the companies are two. The first is related to the firms' size. As stated in Chapter 1, firms with the total employment ≤250 persons are considered as SMEs in this study. This research concerns statistical units classified to the non-financial corporate sector. According to the NACE classification, non-financial entities are all entities of the expected economy: natural persons engaged in individual agricultural holdings, banks, cooperative credit unions, insurance companies and funds, national investment funds, companies, and pension funds, higher education, independent public health care, and cultural institutions with a legal personality, and with the exception of the entire section O, which is: public administration and defense, compulsory social security; section T such as private households with employed employees and households producing goods and services for their own needs; and section U (extraterritorial organizations and bodies). The second is connected with data availability. We use in the sample firms with data available for 11 years continuously. We exclude all firm-year observations without data available on debt (short and long terms), total assets, shareholders equity, sales, and net income. We eliminated the observations of firms with anomalies in their accounts such as negative values in their assets or liabilities. As a result of these conditions, a sample of 612 companies was obtained. The firms of the sample are present in 18 business sectors using the European NACE classification scheme of economic activities, based on the number of firms and the percentage of total sales of the four sectors representing above 90 per cent of total sales in the region and about 70 per cent of the total number of firms. These four sectors of economic activities which dominate in the region are a wholesale and retail trade (G), manufacturing (C), accommodation (I), and construction (F). Table 5.1 shows the distribution of SMEs by sector. The research covers the period from 2006 to 2016, which gives the 11 years of observation of the financial results of selected companies. This period covers three years (2006–2008) before the economic crisis in Greece and the eight years of the adverse economic conditions (2009–2016). In the case of some independent variables like growth, the data for 2005 are also used.

On the one hand, it is quite a long period to observe certain regularities relating to the effectiveness of management skills cycles; on the other hand, there are the years before the economic crisis in Greece, the years of the crisis, and after the crisis. For the second period after 2009, we used the term

Table 5.1 Representativeness of sample data

Sector	*Per cent (in the total number of firms in the region)*	*Per cent (in total sales)*
Wholesale and retail trade (G)	26.2	41.2
Manufacturing (C)	23.2	40.8
Accommodation and food service activities (I)	16.9	3.4
Construction (F)	8.9	4.9
Others	30.2	9.7
Total	**100**	**100**

Source: Own calculations.

adverse economic conditions, since according to the literature it is not clear what should be considered a crisis period. As a result, we obtained a balanced panel dataset of 612 firms and a number of 6,732 firms-years observations. Outlying observations were removed via a 90 per cent winsorization. For all variables, the bottom 5 per cent of the value is set equal to the value corresponding to the 5th percentile, while the upper 5 per cent of the values are set equal to the value corresponding to the 95th percentile.

5.3 Determinants and variables selection

As mentioned earlier, the purpose of this research is to examine the profitability and debt dependency between firms of the sample and to develop a model that will reveal the factors that influence the leverage ratios of SMEs.

The variables chosen to measures the SMEs' leverage ratios along with those chosen to test the factors that affect them are presented and discussed here.

The following dependent and independent variables were calculated for the estimation of the purposes of the study.

This study uses two measures as proxies for firms' leverage: the ratio of the total debt to total assets and long-term debt ratio.

Total debt to total assets: This ratio indicates the percentage of a company's assets that are provided via debt. The ratio is one of the indicators used to measure a firm's financial leverage and financial risk. The higher the debt to assets ratio, the greater the degree of leverage and financial risk.

$$DAR_{j,t} = STD_{j,t} + LTD_{j,t} \Big/ TA_{j,t} \qquad (5.1)$$

where $DAR_{j,t}$ is debt to assets ratio for firm j in period t, $STD_{j,t}$ is short-term debt for firm j in period t, $LTD_{j,t}$ is long-term debt for firm j in period t, and $TA_{j,t}$ is total assets which include all current and non-current assets on the firm's j in period t balance sheet.

Long-term debt to total assets: This ratio is a measurement representing the percentage of a firm's assets that are financed with loans and financial obligations lasting more than one year. In other words, it is a solvency or coverage ratio that calculates a firm's leverage by comparing long-term debt to assets. The higher the level of long-term debt, the more important it is for a company to have positive revenue and steady cash flow.

$$L\_TDAR_{j,t} = {LTD_{j,t}} / {TA_{j,t}} \tag{5.2}$$

where $L\_TDAR_{j,t}$ is long-term debt to assets ratio for firm j in period t, $LTD_{j,t}$ is long-term debt for firm j in period t, and $TA_{j,t}$ is total assets on the firm's j.

Six firm characteristics are used as the determinants of leverage. They are profitability measured by gross margin and return on total assets (ROTA), asset structure which is estimated by capital intensity, firm size, growth, and firm age. These variables are described below.

Gross Margin indicates the gross profit per unit of sale.

$$GM_{j,t} = {TS_{j,t} - CGS_{j,t}} / {TS_{j,t}} \tag{5.3}$$

where $GM_{j,t}$ is Gross Margin for firm j in period t, $TS_{j,t}$ is sales for firm j in period t, and $CGS_{j,t}$ is cost of goods sold for firm j in period t.

ROTA: This is a ratio that measures a company's earnings before interest and taxes (EBIT) relative to its total net assets. The ratio is an indicator of how effectively a company is using its assets to generate earnings before contractual obligations must be paid.

$$ROTA_{j,t} = {EBIT_{j,t}} / {TA_{j,t}} \tag{5.4}$$

where $ROTA_{j,t}$ is return on assets for firm j in period t, $EBIT_{j,t}$ is earnings before interest and taxes for firm j in period t, and $TA_{j,t}$ is total assets for firm j in period t.

Capital Intensity indicates the rate of long-term investment made of the firm.

$$CI_{j,t} = {NA_{j,t}} / {TA_{j,t}} \tag{5.5}$$

where $CI_{j,t}$ is capital intensity for firm j in period t, $TA_{j,t}$ is total assets for firm j in period t, and $NA_{j,t}$ is net fixed assets for firm j in period t.

Firm size is measured as the natural logarithm of assets

$$(LnA_{jt}) \tag{5.6}$$

Growth is measured as percentage change in the value of assets $(Growth_{jt})$.

$$Growth_{jt} = \left(TA_{jt} - TA_{jt-1}\right)/TA_{jt-1} \tag{5.7}$$

Age is estimated by the natural logarithm of the years since the creation of the firm

$$(LnAge_{jt}) \tag{5.8}$$

Trying to analyse the determinants of capital structure of SMEs, we examine the relationship between the size, the age, the tangible assets, and profitability on one side and the leverage of SMEs on the other.

The following measures are considered as dependent variables: total debt to total assets $(DAR_{j,t})$ and long-term debt to total assets $\left(L\_TDAR_{j,t}\right)$. In the first case $(DAR_{j,t})$, we use total liabilities, meaning the aggregate of all debts for which a company is liable (short term, long term). We have to keep in mind that some of the short-term liabilities are not connected with financing, for example, accounts payable, salary payable, and rent payable.

The following measures are considered as the independent variables: gross margin $(GM_{j,t})$, capital intensity $(CI_{j,t})$, return on total assets $(ROTA_{j,t})$, firm size (LnS_{jt}), firm age $(LnAge_{jt})$, and growth $(Growth_{jt})$.

The following regression equation is considered:

$$\begin{aligned} LEV_{j,t} = \alpha + Fir_j + Year_t + \beta_1\, GM_{j,t} + \beta_2\, ROTA_{j,t} + \beta_3\, CI_{j,t} \\ + \beta_3\, LnS_{jt} + \beta_4\, Growth_{jt} + \beta_5\, LnAge_{jt}\, Age + \varepsilon_{jt} \end{aligned} \tag{5.9}$$

where

$LEV_{j,t}$ is dependent variable to DARj,t and L_TDARj,t.

Fir_i captures the firm's specific effects which are not time varying, but rather differ from firm to firm, for example, differences in accounting policy, managerial efficiency.

$Year_t$ captures the year-specific effect which are not unobserved effects constant across firms but varying over time, for example, interest rates.

β is the slope coefficient for independent variables.

ε_{jt} indicates the error term for the observations of firm j in the year t.

α is regression constant.

Moreover, subscript j denotes the studied company and subscript t represents the period.

5.4 Empirical results

In Figure 5.1, we can see the evolution of profitability and business dependence on debt. From the analysis, we observe that till the end of 2009

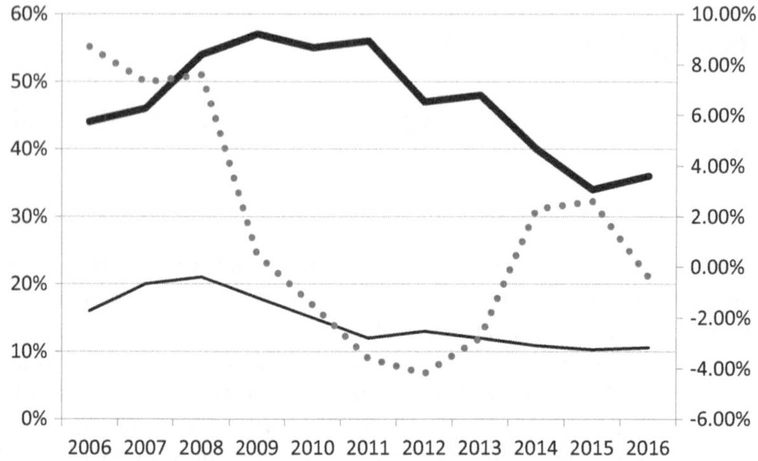

Figure 5.1 Profitability and use of debt, 2006–2016.
Source: Own calculations.
*This figure shows a total debt to total assets ratio shown as a bold black line on the left hand, long-term debt to total assets ratio shown as a black line on the left hand, and return on total assets ratio shown as black dot line on the right hand.

the profitability was on average positive, with a strong downward trend after 2007. During the period 2010–2013, the average profitability was negative. Meanwhile, the average leverage ratio for the whole sample shows an increasing trend until 2011 and then diminishing. It is worth noting that approximately 62 per cent of enterprises participating in the research was using banking debt in financing in the period considered. Comparing the two sub-periods before and during the crisis, we may observe significant credit expansion in the period before the crisis. The increase in total debt in the pre-crisis period was mainly caused by the increase of long-term debt. The impact of the crisis on external borrowing becomes apparent since 2009 when we can note the first decrease mainly in long-term borrowing. The situation changed dramatically in 2010 when for the first time, the change in overall lending by business was negative with a significant reduction of long-term debt and expansion of short-term lending. The initial expansion of short-term lending was caused mainly by the enterprises' efforts to meet the borrowing requirements mainly through short-term borrowing and postponement of their investment plans. Some of the shift also comes from SMEs customers' delayed payment, which causes growing receivables and creates significant problems of firms' liquidity. From 2011, the business access to credit became more difficult and also affected short-term lending. The demand for business loans fell partly because most businesses experienced a decline in sales, business owners had a heightened

Table 5.2 Correlation matrix for analysed variables, all SMEs, two sub-periods

	DAR	*L_TDAR*	*ROTA*	*GM*	*CI*	*Size*	*Growth*	*Age*
				All SMEs (2006–2008)				
DAR	1							
L_TDAR	−0.006	1						
ROTA	0.084	−0.089*	1					
GM	0.034	−0.123	0.308**	1				
CI	0.043**	0.054*	0.204**	0.112*	1			
Size	0.034**	0.215**	0.119*	0.073*	0.043*	1		
Growth	0.012	−0.034	0.278***	0.045	0.013**	0.114	1	
Age	0.032	0.006	0.034	0.202*	0.056	0.013**	0.033	1
				All SMEs (2008–2016)				
DAR	1							
L_TDAR	0.083	1						
ROTA	0.045	0.036*	1					
GM	0.013	0.071	0.244*	1				
CI	0.051**	0.172**	0.182**	0.054	1			
Size	0.123**	0.343***	0.113*	0.311**	0.011*	1		
Growth	0.054	−0.022	0.243**	0.061*	0.007	0.211	1	
Age	0.014	0.063	0.044	0.118*	0.142	0.017*	0.037	1

Note: Variables are defined at the beginning of this section. For every pair of variables, the table provides Pearson's correlation coefficient, t-statistic (*p-value < 0,1; **p-value < 0,05; ***p-value < 0,01).
Source: Own calculations.

level of uncertainty concerning future sales, and they addressed their balance sheet problems by reorganising and scaling down their operations and scaled back their investment plans in a way that reduced their need for external financing. The worsening economic situation in many companies affected their credit standing and limited their access to the credit market.

Table 5.2 shows the results of the Pearson's correlation analyses of the non-crisis period and crisis period for main independent and dependent variables in all surveyed SMEs.

The results of the non-crisis Pearson correlation analysis show that firm size positively relates to both the dependent variables: total debt to total assets and long-term debt to total assets. These relations become stronger during the period of economic constraints. In the case of total debt to total assets, the correlation was 0.034 and was significant at the 0.05 level in the non-crisis period and 0.123 ($p<0.05$) in the crisis period. As far as long term is considered, the correlation increased from 0.215 ($p<0.05$) to 0.343 ($p<0.01$). The results show that the larger firms' access to credit was easier during the two sub-periods. Smaller firms were seen as borrowers with lower creditworthiness. It suggests that firm size resolves the asymmetric information problems since larger firms' financial information may be of higher quality. The difference between the two periods indicates that smaller companies had more difficult access to loans in general and long-term in particular, and access deteriorated during the crisis.

The results in Table 5.2 indicate that there is a positive correlation between tangibility of business assets and use of leverage as depicted by a Pearson correlation value of 0.043 ($p<0.05$) for total debt and 0.054 ($p<0.01$) during the pre-crisis period. During the crisis period, the correlations increased to 0.051 ($p<0.05$) and 0.172 ($p<0.05$) for two categories of leverage ratios. The increase in the correlation of the long-term debt ratio is particularly important and may suggest that firms' fixed assets can be used as a loan guarantee. This conclusion can be confirmed by the fact that the correlation ratio increases especially in the case of long-term loans.

Further, the results show that profitability had a weak positive relationship with leverage expressed as total debt, but the correlations are not significant. When we examine the correlation of long-term debt with profitability, we find a negative correlation for the pre-crisis period with a Pearson correlation value of −0.089 ($p<0.01$). According to the pecking order hypothesis, firms that are profitable are expected to use less debt capital. For the crisis period, positive correlation was found (0.036, $p<0.01$). This means that banks in the period of adverse economic conditions finance profitable companies trying to achieve greater security in returning the loans they have taken.

The results of the two sub-periods correlation analysis show a positive relationship between growth and total debt and a negative relation between this independent value and long-term debt. The correlations are quite weak and not statistically significant.

What is interesting is that the results show a positive and statistically significant relation between ROTA and capital intensity, size and growth with a Pearson correlation value of 0.204 ($p<0.05$), 0.119 ($p<0.01$), and 0.278 ($p<0.01$), respectively, during the non-crisis period and 0.182 ($p<0.05$), 0.113 ($p<0.01$), and 0.243 ($p<0.05$) for the crisis period. This indicates that a higher level of tangible assets, size, and growth could facilitate higher profitability. It should be noticed that the relationship during the crisis period was weaker.

Further evidence indicates that the effect of age on size is positive for non-crisis and crisis periods. This relationship is much stronger during the crisis period but at a lower level of significance.

Table 5.3 reports the results of regression analysis for the specification given by Equation (5.8), which is used to investigate the impact of independent variables on the firm's leverage measured as total debt to total assets and long-term debt to total assets. The result of the Hausman test implies

Table 5.3 Regression analysis of determinants of firm's leverage

Debt assets ratio				
Non-crisis/crisis periods	*2006–2008*		*2009–2016*	
	Beta	*p-Value*	*Beta*	*p-Value*
ROTA	−0.388** (−3.27)	0.001	−0.231* (−3.452)	0.034
GM	−0.187** (−3.451)	0.002	−0.529* (9.512)	0.033
CI	0.181 (3.781)	0.190	0.211** (3.162)	0.001
Size	0.123** (3.756)	0.001	0.435** (3.932)	0.002
Growth	0.054 (0.768)	0.381	0.134 (2.087)	0.072
Age	0.072 (1.346)	0,423	0.073 (1.260)	0.672
Adjusted R^2	0.69		0.71	
Wu-Hausman test	0.00		0.00	
Long-term_debt assets ratio				
Non-crisis/crisis periods	*2006–2008*		*2009–2016*	
	Beta	*p-value*	*Beta*	*p-value*
ROTA	−0,451* (−1,782)	0.043	−0.324 (−3.82)	0.068
GM	−0,037 (−0,275)	0.205	−0.186 (−3.428)	0.106
CI	0.104** (3.98)	0.001	0.276** (3.892)	0.001
Size	0.233** (3.84)	0.002	0.370*** (3.304)	0.000
Growth	0.076** (0.899)	0.465	0.085* (0.923)	0.040
Age	0.123* (3.142)	0.043	0.089 (1.823)	0.067
Adjusted R^2	0.71		0.75	
Wu-Hausman test	0.00		0.00	

Note: Coefficient estimates are in each cell, and T-student are provided in parentheses. ***significant at the level 0.001, **significant at the level 0.05, *significant at the level 0.1.

that the fixed effect estimation is preferable than random effect estimation (Baltagi et al., 2003). The regression analyses are tested to see if there is a presence of autocorrelation and multicollinearity in the data, using the Wu-Hausman test.

The coefficient of ROTA is negative for two regression models and two sub-periods which means that as the return of total assets increases, the firm's total debt and long-term debt decrease. This result is consistent with the pecking order theory, which suggests that firms prefer internal sources of financing when its profitability increases. The relationship is negative (as mentioned earlier), but its significance differs (5 per cent significant for total assets during the pre-crisis period, 10 per cent during the crisis period, and 10 per cent for long-term debt in pre-crisis period) and the related changes in times of a crisis to be non-significant during the years of crisis. It indicates that the relation between ROTA and total and long-term debt is changed in times of crisis.

There is a negative and significant relationship between gross margin and leverage. This indicates that firms with high gross margin use lower total debt in their financing. For long-term debt, this relationship is also negative but not statistically significant.

In the case of capital intensity, we found a positive relationship with high significance in the non-crisis period for total debt and both sub-periods for long-term debt. It shows that firms with a high proportion of tangible assets increase the use of long-term debt or, in other words, banks are more willing to give credit to the firms with a high proportion of tangible assets. According to the results, if capital intensity increases the long-term debt will increase by 10.4 per cent in the non-crisis period and 27.6 per cent in the crisis period. On the other side, the decrease in the capital intensity will cause a decrease in long-term debt by 27.6 per cent. This strong and positive effect of capital intensity on the firm's leverage may be probably explained by the possibility of using fixed assets as loans' collaterals and increasing requirements of banks.

We observe a positive and significant relationship between leverage ratios and firms' size. It shows that a firm increasing its access to the debt is easier. This relationship is even stronger during the time of crisis, especially in the case of total debt. It means that a firm's size is an essential factor of the access to credit not only for long-term loans, but also for short-term loans.

The other variables that have significant effects on firms' leverage are growth and firm's age, affecting it positively. This means that any increase in the firm's growth or age leads debts to grow. The positive relationship between a firm's growth and its leverage implies that an increase in the value of assets causes an increase of the firm's leverage. Moreover, increasing years of the firm's operation increase the firm's leverage, although the last relationship is not statistically significant in the sample.

Based on these results, we conclude that the firm's leverage is more sensitive to the changes in firm's size. Larger firms have easier access to lending. Probably, larger firms are characterised by higher productivity since they can take advantage of economies of scope and scale and thus, can achieve higher profitability.

5.5 Concluding discussion

The crisis had a significant impact on Greek businesses and had a particularly negative impact on their access to external financing. The analysis presented in this chapter attempted to review the evolution of profitability and dependence on the debt of Greek SMEs and the impact of a firm's characteristics on leverage ratios. The underlying rationale for this research is that smooth and sufficient business access to external sources of finance is an essential precondition for firms' survival, and thereby job creation and a prerequisite for the economic recovery. This study uses dataset covering 612 SMEs from the region of Epirus in Greece for the period 2006–2016.

The evolution of the firms' profitability shows a significant decrease over the period considered. At the same time, strong credit expansion is evident before the crisis. The positive change in total pre-crisis debt is mainly due to the increase in long-term borrowing, while short-term borrowing is relatively less volatile over the time. The impact of the crisis on the external borrowing for the investigating enterprises is evident from 2009 onwards. Initially, there were two main trends. On one side, it was the rapid reduction of long-term debt and on the other, increase of the short-term borrowing. It indicates the substitution of long-term with short-term borrowing. However, despite the initial increase of short-term lending, it does not outweigh the negative effect of reducing long-term debt. During the next few years, business access to bank lending becomes even more difficult as the crisis begins to affect the short-term borrowing of businesses. Trying to combine the two trends, we find that the negative profitability of companies as a result of the economic crisis probably have had an impact on the demand and access of enterprises to external borrowing. Analysing the results of the research, we have to keep in mind that SMEs usually have higher funding needs because they are farther away from their efficient scale. As a result, they have relatively higher production costs and lower profit levels, including retained earnings. This limits the possibility of financing from own sources. At the same time, debt financing is relatively more costly to them since they can pledge less collateral and hence, contribute negatively to the firms' available financing.

We also tried to analyse the firms' finance structure with special emphasis on the crisis, thus underlining the relevance of financing and credit conditions to investment and economic activity in turbulent times. The analysis confirms the relevance of most determinants of leverage identified by the economic literature. Results of the research indicated strong and increasing link between the firms' size, capital intensity, and firms' leverage, especially when long-term debt is considered.

Smaller firms have less access to external financing. Also, young firms' access is more constrained. Firms with a higher proportion of tangible assets on the balance sheet, which can be used as collateral and with higher growth concerning percentage change in the value of assets, have higher levels of leverage. The results confirm the effect of the firms' profitability on their leverage. It is in line with the conclusions of the pecking order theory, according to which firms with higher profitability prefer to use internal sources of financing. From the analysis of the crisis period, the strength of the impact of firms' characteristics shows some differences. For example, the results indicate a wider discrepancy between the leverage of firms and the firm's size. The coefficients of the independent variables measuring profits and tangibility are higher during the crisis period, which means that their effects on leverage are relatively more important.

This study is, admittedly, subject to limitations. One of the main limitations is related to the crisis period research. This research focuses solely on firms from one region of Greece. To increase the validity of this study, multiple crisis periods with different causes and implications should be included. Another one of the limitations could be the questionable validity of the accounting data used. Future research is needed to examine whether and to what extent the report in the financial statement's data are manipulated. It would lead to a better understanding of the relationships.

References

Ali, T., 2012, The impact of the sovereign debt crisis on the Eurozone countries, *Procedia – Social and Behavioural Sciences*, Vol. 62, pp. 424–430.

Baltagi, B., Bresson, G., Pirotte, A., 2003, Fixed effects, random effects or Hausman – Taylor?: A pretest estimator, *Economics Letters*, Vol. 79, pp. 361–370.

Berkmen, P., Gelos, G., Rennhack, R., Walsh, J., 2012, The global financial crisis: Explaining cross-country differences in the output impact, *Journal of International Money and Finance*, Vol. 31, No. 1, pp. 42–59.

Bernanke, B., Gertler, M., 1995, Inside the Black Box: The credit channel of monetary policy transmission, *Journal of Economic Perspectives*, Vol. 9, No. 4, pp. 27–48.

Bernanke, B., Gertler, M., Gilchrist, S., 1999, The financial accelerator in a quantitative business cycle model, in Taylor, J.B., Woodford, M., eds., *Handbook of Macroeconomics*, Vol. 1, pp. 1341–1393.

Bernanke, B., 2007, *The Financial Accelerator and the Credit Channel, Board of Governors of the Federal Reserve System*, retrieved on 10/09/2018 from www.federalreserve.gov/newsevents/speech/bernanke20070615a.htm

Ernst & Young, 2013, *Coping with the Crisis, the European Way*, retrieved on 17/1/2014 from www.ey.com/Publication/vwLUAssets/European-Attractiveness-Survey-2013/$FILE/European-Attractiveness-Survey-2013.pdf

European Commission, 2012, *EU SMEs in 2012: At the Crossroads*, retrieved on 29/03/2014 from http://ec.europa. Eu/enterprise/policies/sme/facts-figures-analysis/performance-review/files/supporting-documents/2012/annual-report_eu.pdf

Lallement, M., 2011, Europe and the economic crisis: forms of labour market adjustment and varieties of capitalism, *Work, Employment & Society*, Vol. 25, No. 4, pp. 627–641.

OECD, 2009, *The Impact of the Global Crisis on SME and Entrepreneurship Financing and Policy Responses*, retrieved on 29/03/2014 from www.oecd.org/industry/smes/43183090.pdf

UNIDO, 2013, *World Manufacturing Production: Statistics for Quarter I*, 2013, retrieved on 04/08/2013 from www.unido.org/fileadmin/user_media/Publications/Research_and_statistics/Branch_publications/Research_and_Policy/Files/Reports/World_Manufacturing_Production_Reports/STA_Report_on_Quarterly_production_2013Q1.pdf

6 Recommendations and conclusions

SMEs are critical to European economies. Due to the prominent role of such firms in the economy, the source of finance to support these businesses is crucial. In the last decades, SMEs are considered with increasing interest by European policymakers, public authorities, and economists, who are trying to support them in finding financial resources and establishing cooperative relationships among them to help them remain viable and competitive.

In Greece, 99.9 per cent of businesses have fewer than 250 workers. The critical feature in Greece is the strong presence of businesses with less than ten employees. Although similar to Spain and Italy, this is a much larger share than in Germany and France. However, more significant than the number of companies is the percentage of total employment and value added. SMEs contributed 73.2 per cent of the value added generated within the Greek economy and 86.9 per cent of total employment. In this case, Greece is above the eurozone average, as analysed in Chapter 2. Given their economic relevance, the role of SMEs, their financial performance, and ability to grow and to succeed are essential for the economic development of the Greek economy.

The deep economic crisis that hit Greece is reflected, among others, in the main macroeconomic ratios like the Gross Domestic Product and unemployment and some indicators of the banking sector like deposits, total loans, and non-performance loans. With the real gross domestic product in 2016 almost 25 per cent below its level in 2008, Greek SMEs have borne the brunt of the economic crisis in recent years. In that period, SME employment fell by 27 per cent. Almost one of four of the SMEs that existed in 2008 closed down, reducing the total volume of business, measured in added value, by a third of its 2008 levels. Domestic focus, lack of scale, and limited financial sophistication caused SMEs to be less agile in responding to the crisis; economic crisis decreased firms' profitability and increased needs in finding ways to gain funds.

The financing model of Greek companies is based mainly on bank lending. The average share of bank lending in the overall funding in Greece is much higher than in other countries of the eurozone. In the context of the current crisis, the access to bank loans for SMEs has deteriorated significantly due to lower availability of bank loans that can hamper the exit from a crisis of these firms and the national economy. It is necessary to act harmoniously and in a multidirectional way to boost the growth of the SME sector through the wider use of banking services.

This chapter presents the main conclusions of the analyses carried out in the previous sections of the book and discusses some relevant recommendations. It also contains an admission of some of the issues and problems remaining unsolved in this study, which can be viewed as directions for future researches.

The essential characteristics of the modern environment such as variability, complexity, and uncertainty have a significant impact on the enterprises' decision-making process. SMEs for their efficient functioning must continuously identify changes in their environment and adapt to them. On the one hand, the changes require adaptation processes from the companies, and on the other, the implementation of these processes assumes access to sufficient financial resources. SMEs have very different needs concerning financing compared to large companies. Their growth is affected by the availability and cost of funding. Much of the attention surrounding the growth of small and medium-sized firms is affected by capital structure decisions. There are a plethora of variables which determine the firm's capital structure like industry affiliation, the type of financial system, and the efficiency of the financial system (described in Chapter 1). The degree of asymmetric information depends on the company characteristics. The large firms are characterised by more stable cash flow and lower probability of bankruptcy. So, usually, there is a positive relationship between leverage and the firm's size. According to the theory of financial distress, a firm with a high proportion of tangible assets can use them as collateral and may expect to issue more debt than a firm with a lower proportion of tangible assets, because the former has a lower cost of financial distress in the case of bankruptcy. Unlike large firms, small businesses lack access to public institutional debt and equity capital markets, and the vicissitudes of small business profits make retained earnings a significantly less stable source of capital. As a result, the survival and growth of these firms are conditioned by providing easy access to financing sources and especially to bank loans which are the most important source of external financing. Bigger companies have been rated by the rating agencies and are the preferred investment vehicles of investors seeking higher returns at a time of low interest rates. On the opposite, small enterprises have relatively restricted access to market financing since there is no information on their intrinsic risk (Nahmias, 2015).

Looking at the problem from the general point of view, it should be stated that the company must develop and grow in order to survive in a dynamic and competitive environment. This also applies to crises. The decline in demand for services and goods during the crisis period causes the increase of competitiveness of companies. They are fighting for a shrinking market. One of the ways of persevering these companies in difficult conditions is switching sales to established export markets or finding new ones. However, it requires additional capital expenditures. In the modern environment with rapid technological changes, SMEs play a unique role. Although there is a general belief that SMEs are characterised by lower productivity and higher production costs due to small-scale production, SMEs are well known to generate innovations. However, investment and innovation are not possible without adequate financing. During the crisis, tighter credit conditions, financial instability, and late payment of invoices has deteriorated the liquidity of businesses and therefore intensified their financing needs. A company which is losing its financial liquidity is doomed to liquidation after a period of turbulence. It causes a domino effect on the markets of goods and services. All above-presented factors and processes constitute the primary reasons why improving access to finance is essential to restoring growth and enhancing competitiveness; this concerns both start-ups and existing companies.

Greek SMEs operate within the so-called continental model or bank-based financial system, which is characterised by its less developed capital markets and by the fact that most resources are channelled through financial intermediaries. Capital market in Greece is relatively undeveloped compared to the other European countries. Very few companies in Greece have publicly traded corporate debt. Bank loans are the most significant net source of Greek external financing. This suggests that Greek SMEs have fewer alternative sources of external finance available, which makes them more dependent on bank lending. In this context of a predominance of SMEs in Greece, bank credit takes on much more importance as one of the primary sources of finance. Bank credit is the key to helping small Greek firms maintain cash flow, hire new employees, purchase new inventory or equipment, and grow their businesses.

The financial crisis and the recession negatively affected credit flows to businesses for several reasons. The crisis showed the structural weaknesses that developed in Greece over the past few decades (Gikas and Tagkas, 2010; Karamanis and Hyz, 2016). By comparing results for small business lending with the corresponding results for all business lending, we were able to provide evidence in Chapter 4 whether declines in small business lending were more, or less, severe than declines in total business lending. According to our research, small and medium-sized Greek businesses faced the most significant difficulties in raising funds and tried to substitute external financing by internal sources. In an environment of increased risk aversion and tight financial resources, the size of the business was one of the key factors in maintaining access to finance.

The decrease in the availability of bank credit is due to both demand and supply side factors. Understanding which factors are responsible for the restrained credit to the SMEs is essential to identify whether and what policy actions can help to repair it. Nonetheless, making a conceptual distinction between supply side and demand-side factors in credit markets is relatively difficult. On the demand side, the persistently weak level of economic activity, high uncertainty, low confidence, lack of adequate collateral, lack of information, low credibility, higher financing costs, and the need to reduce the high debt levels have continued to weigh on borrowing. On the other side, a complicated macroeconomic environment characterised by negative GDP growth rates negatively affected the demand for finance, given the difficulty of finding profitable investment projects and the deterioration of the financial health of potential borrowers. When we investigate the supply side, we have to take into account the difficulties facing the banking sector with an increasing share of trouble assets and difficulties Greek banks face in obtaining finance from wholesale financing markets, both the debt and interbank markets, and consequently increasing risk aversion. Banks' perception of the risks associated with potential borrowers led to the credit rationing. The closure of wholesale financial markets to Greek banking industry and financial institutions' consequent risk aversion is greatly hindering companies' access to bank credit, in terms of both the quantity of finance available and the conditions attached to like interest rates, demand for more collateral, and so on. Higher credit costs were putting Greek SMEs at a significant disadvantage. As described in Chapter 4, although Greece is a member of eurozone with the single monetary policy, Greek SMEs cannot compete on an equal base with companies from other countries. Greek lending rates during the period under investigation were 300 basis points higher than those reported for French SMEs and 200 basis points higher than large Greek firms.

From the 1980s to the period of the global crisis, the processes that most influenced the formation of the financial market were deregulation, globalisation, and technological progress. They were based on the liberalisation of the flow of capital and people and the limitation of the restrictiveness of financial regulations. The Greek financial and banking system from the mid-1980s to the 2000s has adjusted to the regulatory framework of the EU. The increase in the profitability of the Greek banking sector was the result of structural changes recorded in this period as well as the favourable macroenvironment. During the last sovereign debt crisis, the Greek banks experienced significant falls in their profitability. The situation of banks according to CAMELS methodology (which was presented in Chapter 4) can be described as 'satisfactory' to 'fair', with the tendency after 2011 and till 2013 to the increasing share of 'less than satisfactory' institutions. One of the main problems was the banks' assets quality measure by the Net Non-performing Assets Ratio. Non-Performing Loans (NPLs) on the bank's loan SMEs portfolio have reached more than 45 per cent. The increase is mainly due to the portion of consumer loans outstanding, which has displayed the most rapid growth rate over the past crisis years. Numerous active loans were being restructured. Intensification of the process of debt restructuring for distressed firms is still necessary. It will allow deploying funds to healthy enterprises. Leaving the problem and putting it back in time causes a worsening situation and limits the access to the credit of healthy companies. This requires the development of procedures with the simultaneous training of banking staff in this regard.

Other features were the continuous decrease in deposits by domestic enterprises and households with capital controls implemented in 2016. In this context, banks have a risk-averse position, and an important part of potential borrowers are excluded from access to finance. During the crisis, banks were required to make a number of changes to their capital structure, including holding more Tier 1 capital and submitting to stress tests. Although Greek banks have received significant funding support, they need to strengthen their balance sheets in order to regain access to market funding.

The characteristic process for this period was the consolidation wave in the form of acquisitions and mergers, which resulted in the increase of concentration in the Greek banking sector. The most important reasons for consolidation processes were the need for the increase of the efficiency by the economy of scale and scope, bank capital enhancement, organisational changes, general cost reduction, reduction of costs of new technology implementation, and diversification of assets and revenues. The number of banks has been declining steadily. The top four banks acquired smaller players and increased their market share of loans from 67 per cent in 2011 to 95 per cent in 2013. As a result of consolidation processes in the Greek banking sector, the number of banks has decreased and the concentration of the market is currently very high. After the consolidation process of the Greek banking sector and rapid restructuring, the entire banking sector has left fewer players in the market (Chapter 4). Smaller lenders, which traditionally provide a much higher share of SME lending than their larger peers were merged. Their customers have struggled to find credit from other lenders. Concentration rate CR 5 reached 94 per cent and is one of the highest in the eurozone. The crisis also caused the need to rescue financial institutions from public funds in order to maintain a well-functioning financing system. In the current context, in which it is essential to recover the investment in order to return to growth and create jobs, the recapitalisation of Greek banks during the crisis was a necessary condition, but not a sufficient one. Although Greek banks have received significant funding support, they still seek to strengthen their balance sheets in order to regain access to market funding.

The crisis has changed the approach to assessing banks, shifting pressure from short-term profitability to long-term stability. Although no one undermines the essence and necessity of a stable financial system for economic development, there is no uniform approach to the concept of stability. There are two different approaches to this concept. The first one prefers to define financial instability (as the antithesis of financial stability) and the second one attempts to define financial stability rather than its absence. Mishkin (1999) states that 'financial instability occurs when shocks to the financial system interfere with information flow so that the financial system can no longer do its job of channelling funds to those with productive investment opportunities'. This definition emphasises the intermediation role of the financial system in providing credit to the real sector and stresses the central role of the asymmetric information in causing financial instability. We can stress in this definition the positive effects, such as the smooth functioning of the financial intermediation system as regards the generation of credit for the economy and the lack of shocks to the problem of information asymmetry. The contribution of banks to generating economic growth, to a large extent by offering effective and countercyclical access to credit, is emphasised in many post-crisis studies.

Benefits from the consolidation processes often become apparent in a long time and are associated with side effects, for example, employment reduction. On the other hand, the increase in the scale of banking activities may cause many negative side effects, for example, limitation of the relationship banking; in other words, the limitation of the close bank relationship (Boot, 2000; Bolton et al. 2013). In the relationship banking, banks develop close relationships with borrowers over time. Such proximity between the bank and the borrower has been shown to facilitate monitoring and screening and can overcome problems of asymmetric information. In this view, relationships emerge as a prime source of an incumbent bank's comparative advantage over de novo lenders. Boot (2000) defines relationship banking as the provision of financial services by a financial intermediary that:

- i Invests in obtaining customer-specific information, often proprietary.
- ii Evaluates the profitability of these investments through multiple interactions with the same customer over time and across products.

The definition emphasises that relationship banking involves borrower-specific – often proprietary – information available only to the intermediary and the customer. Moreover, the information can be used in multiple interactions with the same customer. According to Boot (2000), in recent years, the proliferation of transaction-oriented banking (trading) and direct funding available in the financial markets has started to challenge banks' future as relationship bankers seriously. Transaction-oriented banking focuses on a single transaction with a customer or multiple identical transactions with various customers. In transaction-oriented banking, lending is viewed as arms length finance focusing on that particular transaction rather than being aimed at an information-intensive relationship with a customer (Boot, 2000).

How does bank consolidation affect relationship banking? The bigger the bank's scale, the smaller its interest in small loans, and therefore the smaller support to the segment of small businesses (Peek and Rosengren, 1998). The empirical research so far has focused on small business lending, and finds that mergers and acquisitions involving at least one large bank reduce lending to small businesses, whereas mergers and acquisitions between small financial institutions have a positive impact on small business lending (Berger et al., 1988; Berger and Udell, 1995; Cole, 1998; Strahan and Weston, 1998). This is especially important in the bank-based financial system. Bolton et al. (2013) suggest that relationship banking plays an important role in dampening the effects of negative shocks following a crisis.

The concentration of assets in ever-larger financial institutions is problematic, especially for small business credit because large banks are less likely to make small loans. Generally, large banks use standardised quantitative criteria to assess loan applications from small firms, where small banks favour qualitative criteria based on their loan officers' personal interactions with loan applicants. Similarly, large banks typically have more branches that are more geographically dispersed than do smaller banks and, because of this, large banks need very explicit rules and underwriting guidelines to avoid distortions and to keep loan officers rowing in the same direction. As a result, large banks employ standard criteria, often an individual borrower's score and data obtained from financial statements in the loan decision process – a 'cookie-cutter approach'. By contrast, small banks rely to a greater extent on information and relationship capital about the character of the borrower, a 'character approach', which they use to put any numbers-based assessment of a borrowers' creditworthiness within a broader social context (Cole et al., 2004). This difference in approach to lending has repercussions for small business lending, and the decline in the number of community and cooperative banks has meant small businesses may be losing one of their most reliable sources of credit access.

To understand barriers that face SMEs development and undertake effective assistance, close cooperation between the government, its promotional institutions, and the business community is essential.

During the credit expansion period, the degree of leverage of Greek SMEs increased significantly. The high dependence on external capital has created additional problems for business survival and the deterioration of their financial situation. Perhaps, these developments may also lead to changes in the structure of the Greek economy. Lack of funding, low productivity, accumulation of losses, postponement of investment plans, and lack of liquidity can lead some companies to bankruptcy, increasing the concentration of the market. We can only assume that this may increase the average size of an enterprise, increase in its profitability, and hence its easier access to sources of finance. It cannot be denied that Greek companies have to look for other alternative forms of financing as their use in Greece has so far been extremely limited. In such periods of restricted bank lending, one mitigating factor was the ability of corporations to replace bank credit with alternative sources of financing.

It is often believed that progress towards establishing a banking union may contribute to the reducing funding spreads across countries-members of eurozone. Banking union will create a uniform regulatory framework for banks, establish a single supervisory mechanism, provide a single resolution authority, and protect private deposit holders (Hyz and Gikas, 2018). So, it should create a more level platform for banks to compete across Europe and to reduce spreads for SMEs credit (Bukowski, 2018). However, a banking union cannot be seen as a panacea on the financing problems of Greek SMEs. Also, the information about SMEs creditworthiness and potential will be still very costly and difficult to obtain. So, the problem of asymmetric information is difficult to limit. What about the cost of the information gathering necessary to value SMEs' creditworthiness in Greece?

As discussed in Chapter 4, Greek bank's after the consolidation process reduced branches by 42 per cent and employment by 40 per cent to increase efficiency; as a result, the credit decision process has been centralised. It has two consequences for creditworthiness valuation. The time of the process increased, the process became more formalised and based only on information from financial reports, and at the same time, personal relationships with customers was limited or even excluded. As a result, banks base their crediting on an incomplete picture. On the other side, the information in the financial statements relates only to the results historically achieved by the business. An additional problem in Greece is the continuous lack of financial data availability, delays in data's publishing, and even the total lack of the obligation to publish them. This limits the possibility of their analysis by the institutions and organisations interested in studying the results and trends of the regions or branches of the economy. Due to the lack of transparency regulations and high information asymmetries, transaction costs between borrowers and lenders are very high. Therefore, information transparency, unreliable information, or outdated data information is a serious problem. A frequent phenomenon is the delay of up to two years and even more in the public availability of information. It limits the ability of banks to be a consultant to the business and to create 'win to win' relationships with their clients. The information systems of the various public institutions need to be linked. This problem needs to be solved as soon as possible since it is harmful not only for bank lending, but also access to any other source of external funding. Solving these problems may help to simplify credit applications and valuation procedure and to lowering information costs.

On the other side, large banks in Greece remain small in the European scene. There is a high probability that Greek banks will shoulder less credit risk than before the crisis. Banks' ability to take on new credit risk continues to be affected by ongoing efforts to rebuild capital bases, to lower risk lending portfolios, and reduce costs. Since the bank restructuring process may take quite a long time, the priority should be given to reviving a robust lending channel to healthy SMEs, especially those that are of high potential. It needs targeted actions. Without the restructuring process in the Greek sector of SMEs, they will not be able to compete effectively across the European market. It requires access to a broad mix of funding sources, with an emphasis on alternative funding providers. This subject is out of the scope of this study. There is also a question of knowledge of financial problems by SMEs' owners and managers that make it difficult to understand the negotiations, the creditworthiness assessment process, or the procedures for concluding a loan agreement. To boost the growth of the SME sector through the wider use of banking services, it is necessary to act harmoniously and in a multidirectional way:

1 The policy of the state should take into account the diversity of SMEs regarding the scope and intensity of cooperation with banks. This means the need to develop a strategy to differentiate the range of services for different groups of SMEs, in particular for the smallest companies, including:
   - Creating a system of monitoring of the situation of SMEs regarding their financing needs.
   - Undertaking actions aimed at limiting the costs of borrowing.
   - Strengthening (appointing) intermediaries in the contacts of SMEs with banks, supporting mainly small entities, and not having sufficient knowledge about banking products or criteria for assessing loan applications.
2 In banking policy, the implementation of the following postulates will increase the availability of banking services, especially for SMEs:
   - Improving information (and promotion) on banking products and aiming at breaking the barriers in the cooperation with SMEs.
   - Transition to more relationship banking in order to diagnose and eliminate risk factors jointly with the entrepreneur.
   - Simplification of the credit application assessment criteria.
   - Change in the bank's policy regarding the security of loans.
   - Limitation of the transaction costs of banking services.
   - Supporting the development of institutions whose aim is to facilitate the acquisition of loans by enterprises.

References

Berger, A., Saunders, A., Scalise, A., Udell, G., 1988, The effects of banks mergers and acquisitions on small business lending, *Journal of Financial Economics*, Vol. 50, pp. 187–229.

Berger, A., Udell, G., 1995, Relationship lending and lines of credit in small firm finance, *Journal of Business*, Vol. 68, pp. 51–381.

Bolton, P., Freixas, X., Gambacorta, L., Mistrulli, P., 2013, *Relationship and Transaction Lending in a Crisis*, BIS Working Paper No. 417, July 2013.

Boot, A., 2000, Relationship banking: What do we know? *Journal of Financial Intermediation*, Vol. 9, No. 1, pp. 7–25.

Bukowski, I., 2018, Fundamentals of monetary union and the role of financial markets integration: An overview, in Bukowski, S., eds., *Monetary Unions. Background, Advantages and Disadvantages*, Nova Science Publishers: New York.

Cole, R., 1998, The importance of relationships to the availability of credit, *Journal of Banking and Finance*, Vol. 22, pp. 959–997.

Cole, R., Goldberg, L., White, L., 2004, Cookie-cutter versus character: The micro-structure of small business lending by large and small banks, *Journal of Financial and Quantitative Analysis*, Vol. 39, pp. 227–251.

Gikas, G., Tagkas, P., 2010, Structural changes or possible exit of Greece from the Eurozone, *Acta Universitatis Lodziensis, Folia Oeconomica*, Vol. 239, pp. 67–74.

Hyz, A., Gikas, G., 2018, Financial system supervision: Towards the European Banking Union, in Bukowski, I., eds., *Monetary Unions. Background, Advantages and Disadvantages*, Nova Science Publishers: New York.

Karamanis, K., Hyz, A., 2016, The influence of flexible working on unemployment: Evidence from the Greek labour market, in Petrakis, P., eds., *A New Growth Model for the Greek Economy: Requirements for Long-Term Sustainability*, Palgrave Macmillan, London.

Mishkin, F., 1999, Global financial instability: Framework, events, issues, *Journal of Economic Perspectives*, Vol. 13, No. 4, Autumn, pp. 3–20.

Nahmias, L., 2015, Corporate financing in the eurozone: recent trendsand prospects, retrieved on 18/08/2018 from https://economic-research.bnpparibas.com/Views/DisplayPublication.aspx?type=document&IdPdf=25645

Peek, J., Rosengren, E., 1998, Bank consolidation and small business lending: It is not just bank size that matters, *Journal of Banking and Finance*, Vol. 22, pp. 799–820.

Strahan, P., Weston, J., 1998, Small business lending and the changing structure of the banking industry, *Journal of Banking and Finance*, Vol. 22, pp. 821–845.

Index

Note: **Bold** page numbers refer to tables; *italic* page numbers refer to figures and page numbers followed by 'n' denote endnotes.

For Product Safety Concerns and Information please contact our EU representative GPSR@taylorandfrancis.com Taylor & Francis Verlag GmbH, Kaufingerstraße 24, 80331 München, Germany